dog training
step by step

Also by Michael Tucker
  Dog Training Made Easy
  The Eyes That Lead
  Solving Your Dog Problems

Front cover: Class being taught the retrieve.

dog training
step by step

a new guide for owners and instructors

michael tucker

HOWELL
BOOK HOUSE

New York

Maxwell Macmillan Canada
Toronto

Maxwell Macmillan International
New York   Oxford   Singapore   Sydney

Howell Book House
Macmillan Publishing Company
866 Third Avenue
New York, NY 10022

Maxwell Macmillan Canada, Inc.
1200 Eglinton Avenue East, Suite 200
Don Mills, Ontario M3C 3N1

Macmillan Publishing Company is part of the Maxwell Communication Group of Companies.

Library of Congress Cataloging-in-Publication Data

Tucker, Michael.
    Dog training step by step / Michael Tucker.
        p.   cm.
    Includes index.
    ISBN 0–87605–538–2
    1. Dogs—Training.   I. Title.
SF431.T822   1991
636.7'0887—dc20
                                        91–10214
                                        CIP

Macmillan books are available at special discounts for bulk purchases for sales promotions, premiums, fund-raising, or educational use. For details, contact:

                Special Sales Director
                Macmillan Publishing Company
                866 Third Avenue
                New York, NY 10022

10 9 8 7 6 5 4 3

Designed by Peter Yates
Photography by Alison E. Tucker
Drawings by Michael Tucker
Typeset in Times and Helvetica by Abb-typesetting Pty Ltd
Printed in Singapore

contents

acknowledgements

I wish to thank Senior Constable Robert V. Burton, trainer and handler in the Victoria Police Dog Squad, for his very kind and encouraging remarks in the Foreword he has written for this book.

My grateful thanks go to my daughter Alison for the time and care she gave in taking all the photographs for this book, and to those who brought their dogs along to be photographed, particularly members of the Warringal and Northern Obedience Dog Clubs in Melbourne.

Lastly, but by no means least, my sincere thanks go to Dorothy Wellington, who once again gave her time and expertise in kindly undertaking to type the manuscript.

Note
Measurements in this book are expressed in the metric system, with their imperial equivalents given in parentheses. However, in the case of metres (the most frequently mentioned unit here), equivalents are not given. In fact, 1 metre = 1.09 yards; but for all practical purposes the user of this book can confidently read 'yards' for 'metres'.

I dedicate this book to the people who, during the first half of this century, pioneered dog training—which then expanded beyond all expectations throughout the world.

We are indebted to those men and women for their foresight, interest and devotion in creating a basis upon which we have been able to build, so that trained dogs are now able to work with us, in so many fields, as they have never done before.

foreword

I had the privilege of meeting Michael Tucker in 1975 and immediately the conversation centred on the training of dogs and handlers, and the associated behavioural problems. I was instantly aware that we both shared a passion for dog training, which we have continued to enjoy immensely. The importance of owning an obedient, well-trained dog, and of achieving the best results in training, has always been foremost in our minds.

There are many desirable qualities that an owner should possess to train a dog successfully for obedience, agility and nose work. Among these qualities are infinite patience, perseverance, extrovertness and (perhaps the most important quality) the willingness to succeed. Naturally an instructor must possess these qualities as well, but he must also be able to impart his acquired knowledge to his pupils; in fact, he must be a remarkable communicator. Moreover, we instructors must be able to accept constructive criticism and strive always for perfection, remembering we have an obligation to study dogs so as to learn about how they think, act and respond to certain circumstances. Without these qualities, dog training becomes a chore rather than a pleasurable challenge.

Many fine authors have written innumerable books on dog training and behavioural problems, but none so easy to grasp and follow as the books of Michael Tucker, a dog-trainer for some forty years who knows his subject thoroughly and knows how to impart his vast knowledge, as the many thousands of people that he has trained will readily attest.

Unfortunately, there is no effortless or expeditious way to train a dog, no mathematical formula. However, it has been my experience that the key to successful dog training is *incentive*, and it is the uppermost responsibility of the handler to provide that incentive for the dog in order to enable the training process to succeed.

Michael Tucker in writing this comprehensive training manual, *Dog Training Step by Step*, has in fact provided that incentive for owners, instructors and dogs alike.

Senior Constable Robert V. Burton
Dog Trainer/Handler
Victoria Police Dog Squad

introduction

When I look back over my lifetime as a dog-trainer I always feel indebted to those enthusiastic people who had the foresight and drive to start obedience dog-training clubs for the benefit of their communities. They were pioneers, and their work progressed and expanded beyond all expectations.

The training methods and instructional techniques used many years ago were fairly good, but there was always a desire to make them better. I, like many of my contemporaries, have constantly sought improvement in instructing handlers and training dogs, always believing that there must be an easy, or an easier, way of doing things to get the best results.

I truly love my work as a professional dog-trainer, but I know that there is a limit to what I can do. And so in recent years I have taken to writing books in order to reach out to thousands of other people in Australia and overseas who need help in training their dogs. My first book, *Dog Training Made Easy*, included, among other subjects, the training of dogs in all the obedience exercises found in the Australian obedience trials. This was followed by a companion book, *Solving Your Dog Problems*, which dealt with basic training and the prevention and correction of problems that handlers are likely to encounter with their dogs. But because there is so much to say, I decided to write another book. *Dog Training Step by Step* not only contains a lot more information; it is also written to give guidance and assistance to instructors. This does not mean that the book is just a manual for instructors; on the contrary, it is for everyone who wants to learn how to train and understand his or her dog.

Throughout this book I have placed a great emphasis on basic training. It is so important. When the basics have been taught really well to both handlers and dogs, a good foundation has been laid upon which everything else can be built with virtually no problems. If the basics have not been taught properly, the foundation will be shaky and the structure will crumble.

The book also includes advanced work, agility, jumping tricks, demonstration work, scent work and three chapters on tracking. Tracking is a huge subject on its own, but because it is so fascinating and people are becoming more and more interested in it, I decided to write about it. The relevant chapters explain the theory of scent, how the basics should be laid and how steady progress can be made.

My dog-training career started in 1951 in England when I joined the Epsom and Ewell branch of the Associated Sheep, Police and Army Dog Society. I was still at school and about the youngest member of the club, and I found dog training with my Collie most relaxing in between my studies. Funnily enough I came under great criticism from my school principal, who observed me training one evening from inside the saloon bar of the Glynn Arms Hotel. The landlord of that hotel allowed our club to train on his huge back lawn and, in the winter months, to use the small reception hall for a small fee. When I arrived at school the next day, the principal asked me why I was making a public spectacle of myself training dogs with a lot of old men and women. He went on to tell me that I would not get on in the world doing that sort of thing, and that I should be spending all my time studying school subjects. I brought our conversation to an abrupt end by explaining that I found dog training very interesting and relaxing and suggested that he might like to join the club and bring his Staffordshire Bull Terrier for training in order to make it a better dog!

Two years later I was called up for national service in the Royal Air Force. Having completed my basic training and trade training in the RAF Police, I volunteered to become a dog-handler. I shall always remember the day I was interviewed by Lieut-Col James Y. Baldwin, DSO, in his office at the RAF Police Dog Training Squadron, Netheravon, Wiltshire, where he was the civilian adviser. He asked me how much I knew about dogs, to which I could only reply that I felt that my knowledge was limited but I was eager to learn more. He looked at me with a smiling stare for a while, and said, 'And

so you shall!' He was a grand old gentleman who had had a very distinguished military career, especially during World War I. During World War II he, with the assistance of a few other people and their German Shepherd dogs, demonstrated to the Ministry of Aircraft Production that a patrolling handler and dog could detect and apprehend an intruder on a huge airfield far more effectively than dozens of men merely guarding such an establishment.

I had a wonderful time during my national service and was asked if I would like to instruct during my second year. I accepted gladly and was sent to RAF Cosford, near Wolverhampton, to attend a special two-week crash course for instructors of all technical trades in the RAF. It was called STOM, which stood for School of Training, Organisation and Method. The intense training we received there under very qualified staff made the task of instructing so much easier, and to this day I still use many of the techniques taught to me then.

In 1956 I started a two-and-a-half-year apprenticeship at the Guide Dogs for the Blind Association. I received excellent training there and, having gained all my qualifications, emigrated with my family to Australia in 1967 to take up a post with the Royal Guide Dogs for the Blind Associations of Australia. The knowledge that I gained and was able to impart to others in training guide dogs and blind people over those twenty years was invaluable and the work itself was most rewarding— so much so that I could not let it all go by without writing a book about it in 1984 called *The Eyes That Lead*.

Since 1975 I have continued to live a very full and active life in my own dog-training business. In recent years I have undertaken trips to the USA, Great Britain, West Germany and Sweden, visiting many professional dog-training establishments in order to learn more. During those trips it has always been a great pleasure for me to help people when I have been invited to conduct seminars for large groups or take small groups in dog clubs.

Amongst the obedience dog-training clubs and the service and charitable organisations I have worked in or visited over the years, I have seen some excellent instruction and handling. Regrettably, I have seen at other places very poor standards of training which, I am sorry to say, were a reflection on the instructors and the instruction given. In some cases I have been appalled by what I have seen. At one club I visited I never heard any of the instructors praise the handlers for anything they did well; on the contrary, they often criticised them and told them how sloppy they were. I have also known of some instructors who would say to new beginner classes that unless they were going to train their dogs for obedience trials, they would not be interested in training them. That sort of talk is deplorable. The instructors' first aim should be to teach the handlers how to train their dogs. Whether or not some of the handlers might later wish to train for competitions should be left entirely up to them.

Years ago I met one instructor who was most rude to the handlers in the way he criticised them. Some weeks later he admitted to me that he had never trained a dog himself!

I always feel very sorry for those who declare that they have no need to attend special dog-training courses, seminars or evening talks because they know it all. How foolish to say anything like that. No-one can ever know it all, and those who believe they do are often the very people most in need of attending such events.

I hope therefore that with this book I will be able to continue to help thousands of people in the canine fraternity all over the world. I also hope that those who have read it and absorbed it will in turn help others to become responsible, understanding and capable dog-owners.

1

obedience dog-training clubs

I wonder if you have ever thought what types of people join obedience dog-training clubs, even if only for a short time. Well, if you asked them, the vast majority would tell you that they joined a dog club in order to learn how to train their dogs, so that they could have well-behaved pets of which they could feel proud. I think you would further discover that most had been prompted to take up dog training because their dogs had become increasingly difficult to handle, and some would admit that their dogs were completely out of hand. Others would tell you that they wanted to do the best thing for their dogs and for themselves by learning how to train dogs before they encountered difficulties and problems. This is a sensible attitude: it shows both foresight and the realisation that when it comes to dog training it is the owner's responsibility to do something about it, instead of leaving it and hoping for the best. Those who say 'She'll be right, mate' and hope for the best often end up regretting it and wishing they had trained their dogs when they were young and easier to handle.

Dog-training clubs tend to have a huge annual turnover of members. One of the reasons for this is that many sign up with all good intentions, but for various reasons do not do their homework, do not get results, and after one or two attendances are never seen again. I always feel that this is a great pity.

As for those people who do stay, it is always interesting to know why, and what it means to them. A small percentage like to train well in order to compete in trials, especially if they have dogs that show promise in that field. This means of course that they have to be very dedicated, and must have the time and motivation to travel up and down the country to attend trials.

Other people are not interested in competitive work, but are still interested in training their dogs to do all the exercises laid down in the trials, and more. You will often find that many of them are enthusiastic members in the clubs' demonstration teams; they do a fantastic job promoting their own clubs and obedience training generally, and provide good entertainment for the public at various community functions.

There are also those members who like attending dog-training classes in order to relax and do something completely different from what they do every day. The companionship of their dogs and the interest they share with other members help them to come together and enjoy the social side of club life, not only in their own clubs but within the canine fraternity generally. Frequently these members put a lot back into their clubs, by sitting on committees and subcommittees and performing all manner of duties essential to the running of an efficient and highly regarded dog-training club.

Among the people who stay in dog clubs for some time, there are a few who are invited and take up stewarding in rings, especially if their interests lie in competitive work. Many of them, with the schooling they have had from numerous judges, take the next step and take up judging. Judging requires not only a full knowledge of the rulebook but also a watchful eye and an intimate knowledge and understanding of how a dog works.

Finally, out of all of those dedicated people, there are a few who would like to take up instructing. When they do, they have the opportunity of helping new members and thereby giving something special back to the club in return for the training they themselves received. At the same time anyone who takes up instructing will learn much more in training others than is possible in training only one's own dog.

I have been training dogs for nearly forty years, and in that time I have trained only four dogs of my own: three Border Collies, and the German Shepherd dog I have at present. Naturally, I have gained a lot of experience training and working these four dogs over the past four decades; but in addition, I have trained more than 6000 dogs and handlers. Of these, 176 were guide dogs and their owners, and I can honestly say that training them gave me the greatest rewards—simply because I, like my former colleagues, could train and provide a new means of mobility for men and women who were blind.

It goes without saying that I continue to derive great satisfaction from helping people train their dogs to be happy and well-behaved companions. So if you have the chance to instruct, take it. Nothing is difficult, when you know how. And that is just what I intend to show you throughout this book.

2

introduction to obedience

I well remember my first visit to the dog club which was to pave the way for my future as a dog-trainer and instructor. It was the only dog-training club for many miles around—indeed, there were not too many in Great Britain at that time. There were only two classes: one for beginners and the other for the more experienced. There were about twenty members with quite an assortment of breeds, from a Dachshund to a Pyrenean Mountain Dog.

The instructor stood in the middle shouting out all the orders—'Forward!' 'Halt!' 'Forward!' 'Right-about turn!'— while the handlers and their dogs walked around in a circle. Dogs were pulling, handlers were struggling. Some dogs were barking, others were jumping around all over the place; some were stubborn and refused to budge, others were aggressive and tried to grab the dog in front by the tail. They were all shapes and sizes: big ones, little ones, fat ones, thin ones, long ones, short ones, slow ones, fast ones! You name it, the club had it. And yet everyone seemed to be interested and determined. They were what you might call 'real doggy people', but then the English are, aren't

they? (And I say that being English myself.) Some of the handlers actually looked just like their dogs, and a few even dressed in such a way as to match in with their dogs' colours!

I believe I did the right thing in attending that evening without my dog. I just wanted to see what went on. Although the beginner class was something of a fiasco, the more experienced class was showing promise. Dogs were heeling fairly well, their stays were quite good and so were their recalls. A few dogs were retrieving and a couple of the more experienced dogs did send-aways. I watched intently that evening, and made up my mind to join the club. I took my dog along the following week.

The tuition we were given in those days was nowhere near what is taught in many clubs today. Nearly every week new members would join with their dogs, without first having observed the classes at work. Consequently a lot of time was spent showing new handlers what to do while others who had attended several times had to wait patiently. I guess we thought the standard of instruction was satisfactory, but I for one would certainly not consider it satisfactory by today's standards. Why?

Well, first of all, we did not know very much. We all tried to do the best we could, but the methods used in those days were not all that good. We had no trained instructors. The people who taught us had succeeded in training their own dogs to do the exercises, but they did not have the expertise in explaining and demonstrating to others how they should go about it. There was no simple dog psychology explained, and voice control was not taught enough. The running of classes was not very efficient and results were gained more or less by trial and error. Nevertheless, I still praise those people for having the interest and willingness to instruct. Someone had to; we had to make a start somewhere.

There was one exercise which was rightly taught very early in the training, and that was the retrieve. The main reason for this was that it was in all the obedience competitions, and of course still is in Great Britain today. So we had to get on with the job quickly, because without it there was little point in entering the competitions. Even today I urge dog clubs to teach this exercise early to those who want to compete in obedience trials. In Australia and the USA dogs can gain their first title of CD in novice trials where the retrieve does not exist; but if handlers wish to go further by entering Open and Utility trials, where dogs do have to retrieve, they may well be faced with difficulties. I will say more about this later.

Well now, how can we make the training better so that the instructor's task is made easier, the handlers can understand everything clearly, and the dogs can be trained effectively in the shortest possible time?

What I have been suggesting to dog-training clubs for many years is: Start beginner classes on the first training day of the month, but just a few days prior to that day arrange for the instructor to give the new handlers a lecture. Much can be gained by this. The instructor can be introduced to the class. The new members can get to know their instructor, learn the theory of dog training, the basic principles, the exercises they will be taught, the correct and incorrect way of putting a slip-collar on a dog, and many other things (Figs 1 and 2). They can ask questions and the instructor can get a fairly good idea of what the dogs will be like when he or she meets them at the first training session. The one big advantage of such an introductory lecture is that handlers can feel much more at ease and are far better able to concentrate on what the instructor talks about than if they had their dogs with them. With their dogs present, they would be lucky if they absorbed a quarter of what was said, because they would be spending most of their time trying to control them.

Now a question that is immediately asked in connection with that system is: What if new members want to join the club just a few days after the instructor has started the latest beginner course? In answer to that, new members should be politely informed that they will be more welcome to start in the *next* beginner class, which is to commence in less than a month's time. The vast majority of new members can readily understand the reasons for this policy, and it will after all be in their interests to wait that little while and start with others from the beginning.

Fig. 1. The correct way of putting on a slip-chain collar. Note that the fine links run from the ring attached to the leash, through the other ring, and continue over the top of the dog's neck so that the collar loosens automatically when the leash is relaxed.

Fig. 2. The incorrect way of putting on a slip-chain collar. The fine links are going through the ring and underneath the dog's neck. In this case the collar will not loosen when the leash is relaxed.

But even though they may have to wait, they should be welcome to attend the club so that they can at least watch the classes being trained. It could also be arranged that they bring their dogs, not to train them but to allow them to acclimatise themselves to the dog-training environment. This makes it much easier for many dogs when they do come for training a week or so later.

When I trained at the RAF Police Dog Centre during my national service, there were new courses of between four and eight handlers with dogs starting nearly every week, and each instructor took his course through from beginning to end. What everyone liked about the course was that a lecture was given just prior to most of the practical training sessions with the dogs. Everything seemed to be well organised to ensure that handlers and dogs received the best training in a carefully planned programme that dealt with everything step by step. Naturally there had to be room for flexibility and this was left up to the discretion of the instructor. I would also like to say here that the standard of training in that school has continued to improve over all these years and I feel sure that it will continue to be recognised as one of the world's best.

I have always believed that it is very important for beginners to have the one instructor until the basic course has finished. While the instructor gets to know the handlers and their dogs, their difficulties if any, and the rate of progress of each, the handlers and dogs get to know the instructor and gain confidence in that person. In contrast to this, just consider for one moment how confusing it can be for a class of handlers to have a different instructor nearly every week. Oh yes, it does happen, and I am sure many readers who have attended dog-training classes have had this unfortunate experience. It is also very difficult for the instructor to suddenly take on an unfamiliar class, and much time is wasted establishing what exercises the handlers are doing and what difficulties they have in managing their dogs.

Whenever I hold a special weekend dog-training course for a large group of up to twenty, I always give a lecture an evening or so before the practical working sessions. These interested and keen handlers often come from different clubs and I am well aware that they have all been trained slightly differently. In attending the lecture they get to know what I am going to do in the practical work, and how I am going to do it. They always ask many questions, and in answering these I throw in my own questions as well. By doing it this way I can find out how much they know.

At the conclusion of such a lecture I always say that I shall look forward to seeing them with their dogs on the training day at the appointed time, and I further ask if they would try to arrive at the training ground about ten to fifteen minutes earlier in order to relax with their dogs, so that when we actually start both they and their dogs will be calm. This is very important, because if a handler rushes there, gets the dog out of the car quickly, runs across to where the class has assembled and gasps in a hot and bothered state 'I'm sorry I'm late', he or she is likely to transmit the tense feelings to the dog.

So when the first practical training session is held, it is very important for the instructor to keep calm and transmit that calmness to the class. The instructor can do this by welcoming the whole class and then quietly inviting the handlers to come forward one by one, with their dogs on loose leads, so that the dogs can sniff and meet the instructor. I always say dogs fall into three main categories: most are friendly, a few can be nervous, and occasionally you will meet an aggressive one. It is very important that the instructor allow a dog to settle down in its own time. If the instructor approached the dogs, the suspicious ones could become very afraid, and some with even a small degree of pure, protective or nervous aggression could bite.

The instructor should also ensure that the class is well spread out to avoid any possible fights between dogs. Dogs that feel hemmed in by other dogs will often panic and start to snap. The instructor should show the handlers how to talk to their dogs in order to keep them calm; how to correct them if necessary with the reproof 'No!' in an abruptly deep tone of voice, followed immediately by a physical jerk on the leash; and how, as soon as the dog responds, to give it quiet slow praise, 'Good dog'. The instructor can teach this effectively to everyone only by pure example, using a quiet voice with the right intonation for everyone to copy, and in fact to imitate if they can. If the instructor shouts, the handlers are likely to do the same, and it is highly likely that the shouting will stir the dogs up and they will become harder to control.

The next thing to do before even thinking about showing the handlers heelwork is to show them how to walk their dogs freely on the leash, slowly across the training ground. This gives the dogs, and some-

Fig. 3. When a dog pulls while walking freely on the leash, the handler should say 'Steady', jerk firmly back on the leash and immediately relax it. As soon as the dog responds it should be praised quietly and slowly 'Good dog'. Note that with one foot straight forward most of the handler's body weight is on the other foot, which is bent slightly. This prevents the handler from toppling forward.

Fig. 4. When correcting a dog that pulls, the handler should never stand with feet together and lean forward. The dog would only have to give an extra pull to have its handler on the run, or falling face-downwards!

times the handlers as well, time to settle down. Most dogs pull on their leashes and this problem is quite easily solved if the instructor asks to borrow a dog, preferably one that pulls, and demonstrates to the class by walking along in company with the owner. When the dog pulls, the instructor should explain to the handler how to say 'Steady' in a quiet, slow way, give a firm backward jerk on the full length of the leash and *immediately* relax it; and as soon as the dog responds to praise it quietly and very slowly 'Good dog'. It is important that the instructor explain to the whole class why 'Steady' and 'Good dog' should be said in a quiet, slow way. It is of course to keep the dog calm. If the same words were shouted quickly, the dog would probably get all stirred up and start pulling again. It's not what is said but how it is said that really matters.

It is also very important that the instructor show all the handlers how to use their bodies in carrying out this simple correction. With one foot straight forward, most of the body weight should be placed on the back foot with knee bent slightly. Thus full use can be made of body weight, instead of total reliance on muscle power in the arms (**Fig. 3**). It is equally important for the instructor to tell people what not to do—which is to stand with their feet together, lean over forwards and try to jerk the dog back. This can be

explained and demonstrated without a dog or leash. By standing with the feet together and leaning forwards, in such a way that the class can have a side view, the instructor can show clearly that if a dog gave an extra pull its handler would topple forwards because the body would be leaning that way with no foot straight out in front as a firm prop—with possibly disastrous results (**Fig. 4**)! These are the sorts of things an instructor needs to demonstrate to handlers in the very first practical lesson, so that they can make it easy on themselves and prevent accidents.

After this simple means of control is taught in free-walking a dog, whereby it is allowed to walk anywhere around the handler so long as it doesn't pull, I am always pleased to hear from handlers, when I see them a week later, how pleased they are that their dogs can be free-walked on their leashes without pulling. They tell me how enjoyable it has become to take their dogs out for walks, whereas previously it had been unpleasant because their dogs were taking them!

So you can see from the outset that a great deal depends upon the instructor, whose job it is to explain everything simply and briefly, to demonstrate well, to assist handlers individually, to use the voice well, to show the wrong ways too (explaining why they are wrong), and above all to keep the class calm.

3

heelwork

The main purpose of teaching any dog to heel is to get its respect. On this exercise hinge all the other exercises in obedience. Therefore it is vitally important that this exercise be taught really well by the instructor. If it is not, many problems—for instructors, handlers and dogs—can develop in the future.

The instructor should introduce handlers to heelwork by opening with a short remark of praise, which makes them feel pleased:

'Well now, handlers, you all now know how to walk your dogs freely on loose leads and I think you have learnt that very well in quite a short time! Now I am going to show you how to get your dogs to heel strictly on your left-hand side. You may wonder why it has to heel on your left and not your right. Well, when man first started hunting with the dog and the gun, he normally carried his gun in his right hand. So he heeled his dog on his left side, so that it wouldn't get in the way of the gun. And to this day throughout the world you'll find that virtually all working dogs, show dogs and dogs trained like yours in obedience, work on our left. It doesn't matter if you are left-handed or right-handed—you'll have to use both hands anyway in training your dogs.

'All we are going to teach the dogs to do today is, starting from a sitting position beside you, to accompany you forward on the command "Heel", to heel generally for a short distance and then come to a halt on the command "Sit". We will do that a few times and we will make it very easy for the dogs by walking in dead straight lines over the training area.'

That is all the instructor needs to say in giving a brief explanation of the exercise. Further points can and should be explained later.

Now the exercise needs to be demonstrated, but how and with what? There are several possible methods, but they do not all necessarily give the best tuition to the handlers. Let's have a look at them.

1. The instructor could just stand still and tell handlers what to do. This is most unsatisfactory, and it is quite wrong to expect beginners to remember all the instructions, let alone perform them.
2. A slightly better way is for the instructor to demonstrate with an imaginary dog. But this leaves too much to the imagination of the totally inexperienced handlers. The method can sometimes be used later, when they are more experienced.
3. The instructor could demonstrate with his or her own dog. But this dog would have been trained already and would probably not put a foot wrong. Hand-

lers would not be able to see how faults should be corrected. Personally, if I used this means of demonstrating I would feel I was cheating. I could well imagine some handlers say to themselves, 'Well yes, that looks very nice, Michael Tucker, but then you specially selected that dog when it was a puppy, and as a professional trainer you trained it gradually as it grew through puppyhood. Consequently, you have had no problems, and it works beautifully now. But we have only recently acquired our dogs, some of which are adults, from such places as the lost dogs' home and similar animal shelters. In many cases our dogs are unknown quantities. We have no idea what sorts of homes and conditions they have lived in or why they became lost and were never claimed. Perhaps some were just dumped by their callous, irresponsible owners. Michael Tucker, I would like to see you handle *our* dogs!' Well, I believe they would be quite justified in thinking this way.

The only time I would use my own dog to demonstrate is when handlers wanted to see a trained dog work so that they could get a good idea of what they were ultimately aiming for.

4. Another way of demonstrating is to have an assistant who can actually demonstrate with a dog while the instructor describes everything to the class. But once again the dog being used would be trained and unlikely to make errors, and that is exactly what handlers want to see and learn how to correct. However, this way of demonstrating is ideal in certain facets of work, especially with more advanced work like tracking, where the instructor can stand with the handlers and describe what is going on while they

watch an experienced handler and dog following a track. This will be covered in a later chapter.

5. By far the best way to demonstrate is for the instructor to ask the class if anyone would care to lend a dog for a little while, and preferably a dog that has never been taught to heel—or one that has but still tries to pull ahead.

I have found that there is always someone who will lend me a dog—in fact, several people will volunteer their dogs, saying, 'Yes, you can have mine. He won't do a thing *I* tell him to do!' And as soon as the handler hands the dog over to me, I notice a look of relief on the person's face, as much as to say, 'Thank goodness you've got him for a bit. It'll give me a rest.'

How should the transfer take place? Firstly, the instructor should thank the handler for offering the dog and ask the handler to bring it quite freely on the leash and allow it to sniff the instructor. The instructor should then discreetly take the leash and ask the handler to *spell* the dog's name (assuming it is not already known). The handler should not return to the class yet, for if this happened the dog would more than likely follow its owner, but should remain in the same position until the instructor captures the dog's attention and craftily leads it away in great fun during which he or she, as prearranged, signals to the handler to retreat.

The instructor, now knowing the dog's name, can very joyfully say something like 'Sam! Hello, Sam! Oh, you lovely boy, this way, old boy! Oh, what a lovely boy you are! What a clever boy!' It's amazing how many a dog can be led away from its owner by an instructor chatting to it by name, in a funny, joyful-way. Most dogs love it, they really do.

Although each dog had made the instructor's acquaintance when the class first assembled, this acquaintance has now been taken one step further by the instructor taking the dog.

With handlers and dogs standing in one line abreast of each other, the instructor should stand a few metres in front of the handler on the right-hand end, facing across the front of the class **(Fig. 5)**. Holding the handle of the leash in the right hand, and holding the leash at a point further down, also in the right hand, the instructor should explain to the class that it is important for the right hand to be kept in the centre of one's body just below the belt line, so that the rest of the leash, between the right hand and the dog's slip-

collar, is hanging down in a loop. This part of the leash must be kept slack **(Fig. 6)**. If it is too short and becomes tight, the natural reaction of the dog is to pull because it feels the heavy load on the other end of the leash. The left hand should be kept off the leash, and should be used only for corrections—immediately the correction is made the left hand should let go of the leash. If a handler holds on to the leash with the left hand, and even if a little tension occurs on the leash, the dog will start to pull. This is a very common fault in elementary obedience **(Fig. 7)**.

Just before demonstrating, the instructor should explain how the forward is going to be done and how the dog will be corrected if it goes too far ahead, i.e. out

Fig. 5. When demonstrating forward, heel and sit, it is best for the instructor to walk across in front of the class from the right-hand end so that the handlers can see everything from the side view. The instructor can watch the dog while explaining the heelwork to the class.

Fig. 6. It is very important that the leash be held correctly, and that it hang down in a loop between the handler and the dog.

Fig. 7. If the leash is too short, or if even a slight pressure is applied on it with the left hand while walking, it can so easily cause the dog to pull forwards.

of the true heel position. The instructor could explain like this:

'Handlers, you will see how the dog is sitting beside me and how I have the leash held correctly in my right hand. My left hand, which is my correcting hand for it is the hand nearer the dog, is hanging down loosely beside me ready to be used if necessary. I've made the decision to go forward, I have the dog's attention, I'm prepared to go. I shall give the command in an inviting, quiet tone: "Sam, heel". This will immediately be followed by my bodily action of stepping forward. The dog, seeing me step forward, will want to accompany me. It will respond by moving one of its front paws forward and as soon as I see that response I will immediately give praise in a very pleasing, sincere tone, "Good dog", in order to assure the dog that it has done the right thing, at the right time, in the right place.

'Now, I have no doubt at all that when we have walked only a few steps, the dog will start to go too far ahead. As soon as I see this happen I shall

correct it immediately by taking hold of the clip part of the leash with my left hand, thumb on top, commanding in a quiet but firm voice, "Heel!", jerking backwards very quickly and horizontally along the dog's back and as close to my left leg as possible, and *stopping*. I shall immediately let go of the leash with my left hand, stand up and keep quite still. By doing that, I will have refused to go any further, as if to say, "Now look here, Sam, you're not going to take *me* for a walk. You wait there until I invite you to accompany me." I shall remain there for a few seconds, and provided Sam has not moved, I'll start again. Now ladies and gentlemen, I'd like you to watch this very carefully indeed. Here we go! Sam, heel. I step forward, he responds. Good dog. Everything is OK, but now look, he's going ahead. I grab the clip part of the leash, say "Heel!", jerk back, let go and stand quite still. Now we will start again.'

This simple method of training dogs to heel does not take long, and by explaining and demonstrating it in a straight line across and in front of the class, the instructor's task is made easier and the handlers can learn all the better. Having gone right across in front of the class, the instructor can return to the starting position and demonstrate once more, this time explaining how to get the dog to sit.

'Well, handlers, as you saw for yourselves, after a few corrections Sam learnt to heel quite well in that very short time. I will now demonstrate the heelwork to you again, and this time I'll show you how to sit a dog. You will all be able to see from the side view how I use my leash and hands and how the dog responds by bringing its hind legs up to its forepaws as he comes into the sit position. I shall do this a few times as I walk slowly across in front of you all. Sam, heel! Good dog! Having decided what I am going to do, and having Sam's attention, I prepare by putting the clip part of the leash into my right hand and, placing my left hand over his hindquarters, I now give

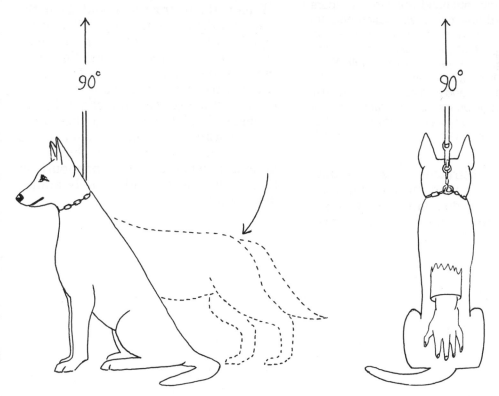

Fig. 8. The correct way to sit a dog. It is most important to hold the leash near the clip, with the right hand, at 90° to the ground and directly above the dog's head, while the left hand pushes the dog's hindquarters down and forwards so that its hind feet come up towards its front feet. If the leash is pulled back at an angle as the hindquarters are pushed down, the dog will feel as if it is being tossed backwards and will either resist or sit crookedly.

Fig. 9. By placing the left hand with thumb to the left and fingers splayed out, pressure from the palm of the hand can be applied. Note that even from this back view the leash must be held at 90° to the ground. If it is held at any other angle the dog will sit crookedly.

the command, "Sit!", hold the leash at 90° above his head and at the same time push down and forwards with my left hand, with my thumb facing to the left. It's the same action as throwing a cricket ball underarm. The dog responds and I praise saying, "Good dog, good boy, very clever boy, oh you good dog!" and at the same time I stroke the dog slowly and gently in order to keep him calm and attentive. I also let go of the clip part of the leash with my right hand so that there is no tightness on his collar, and you will see that I still have the other two parts of the leash in my right hand, and I'm all prepared to go forward again. You will notice also that both my feet are facing straight ahead and not into the dog, which can cause it to turn away towards the left, a very common fault. Watch again carefully how I prepare for the next sit as I'm walking along, and also watch how I bend my knees, which helps me to keep facing straight and to keep my body weight above my feet as I push Sam's hindquarters down and forwards.' **(Figs 8** and **9)**

When the instructor has sat the dog a few times, it is then most important to show how the dog must be dismissed so that it knows the short lesson is over:

'For Sam to understand that the heelwork is over and he can relax, I have now got to give him a command or phrase and a visual signal with both hands in order to dismiss him, and as soon as I have done this we are back to free-walking again. It's just like a schoolteacher dismissing a class of children so that they can go out into the playground to play until the bell goes again. Similarly, when we say "Heel" to the dog, it will soon understand that on that command the next lesson begins.'

Finally the instructor should thank the owner for the use of the dog. When handing it back I always think it is nice to hear an instructor pass some complimentary remark about the dog, such as 'Thank you so much for the loan of your dog, Jean, he took to me so well and showed great willingness'. Not only is the instructor expressing appreciation; also, it makes the handler feel proud of her dog. Such complimentary remarks help tremendously in developing a warm and friendly atmosphere within a class.

4

practical work with the class

Having explained and demonstrated how to go forward, heel and sit, it is now up to the instructor to 'sell' it by assuring the handlers that it is all quite easy and inviting them, one by one, to have a go:

'Well, you see how easy it all is. Now how would you all like to try a little heelwork yourselves? There's nothing to worry about. You'll find that everything will fit into place in a very short time. I shall prepare you for everything and we'll do it one at a time, but as each person does it I would like you all to watch, because you'll be surprised how much you will learn by watching.

'Fred, as you are on the right-hand end of the class, perhaps you would like to start with that lovely, fluffy dog of yours. That's good! You've got her sitting nicely beside you and you are holding the lead quite correctly. When I say "Forward", quietly invite her "Sally, heel", step forward slowly, and as soon as she responds praise her quietly and sincerely "Good girl!". I only want you to walk in a straight line for about 20 metres and finally to bring her into the sit position. If, while you're walking, she goes too far ahead, correct her like I did with Sam a few minutes ago. To help you keep straight, aim towards that tall tree in the distance. Treat that as your reference point. Now watch carefully, everyone. Are you ready, Fred? Forward!'

Because there are quite a few things to remember and watch out for, it is very important that the instructor help each handler to say the right words and do the right things. So as soon as Fred says 'Sally, heel', the instructor should say 'Now step forward'. When the dog responds by moving her first paw forward, the instructor should say in a quiet, sincere, pleasing tone 'Good girl!' so that Fred can copy the instructor's voice. Before long the bitch will start to go too far ahead. The instructor must tell Fred to correct her in the fewest words possible:

'Correct her! Grab the clip part of the leash! Say "Heel". Jerk back horizontally with your left hand. Let go. Stand up and keep quite still for a few seconds. That was a good correction, Fred. Now quietly start again. Yes, that's going very well.

'Fred, now prepare to sit her. Put the clip part of the leash in your right hand. Put your left hand over her hindquarters. Now say "Sit!". Hold your right hand above her head as you push down and forwards with your left hand as if you're throwing a ball underarm. Now release the clip part of the leash and keep praising her, "Good girl. There's a good little girl. Very good. Very clever".'

It is important for the instructor to say these words so that the handler can hear and try to imitate both the words and the voice. The rest of the class should also be able to hear, and the best place for the instructor to be is at the left side of the handler and dog, and walking backwards so as to be able to talk to the rest of the class **(Fig. 10)**. If the instructor faced forward, the rest of the class would feel as if they were being ignored.

'Well, did you see that, everyone? Didn't Fred do a good job? I told you it's easy. You've seen it with your own eyes. It was a nice smooth take-off at the forward, the correction the dog received for going too far ahead was effective, and finally you could all see how easy it was to sit a dog provided one prepares well for it while walking along. Now I want you to watch how Fred dismisses the dog. All right, Fred, tell her to "Go free", and use both your hands from under the point of her chin and signal to her that she can go free by splaying them out to the left and right. As she does so now, praise her. Now if you'd like to return to the class, Fred, and relax and watch the others, I shall take the next person through.'

And so it goes on. Each handler has individual tuition that lasts for a short time; but the whole class is receiving instruction all the time provided they watch intently and the instructor is positioned correctly, talks to them and glances at each one so that they all feel they are part of the team working together. So if the class consists of, say, twelve handlers and dogs, each will receive individual training and will see and hear it another eleven times.

I think that about six dogs in a beginner class is an ideal number for any instructor, but sometimes one can have twice that many or more. Regardless of the number,

I believe they all need to have that little bit of individual attention.

In an all-breeds dog-training club, there are going to be dogs of all sizes, from a little Chihuahua to an Irish Wolfhound. Some breeds will have long legs and short bodies, and others will have very short legs and long bodies. Some will be naturally quick, others slower, depending on physical structure. You will see them all develop their own ways of sitting.

In addition to all the peculiarities of the dogs, the characteristics of the handlers will also differ. Some will be quick to learn, others slow. Some will have very good coordination, others a distinct lack of it. Some will be natural handlers, others awkward. But it is up to the instructor to observe and become aware of them, and to help the handlers train their dogs to a standard with which they are happy.

I consider the first obedience lesson to be the most important, for both handler and dog. In this first lesson handlers learn about the first principle of training, with its four main points of *Command*, *Action*, *Response* and *Praise*. When they have learnt these points in that order, they can apply the principle to everything they teach the dog to do, or not to do, in the future. They will also start to realise how important it is to use the hands, feet and body correctly; how vital the use of the voice is going to be as a means of control; how they must keep their eyes on their dogs, keep calm and keep their dogs calm; how they need to be consistent and firm at all times; and above all, how they can really enjoy what they and their dogs do together.

In this first lesson, a foundation is being laid, a foundation on which to build in subsequent weeks and months and perhaps years. With a good foundation laid, it

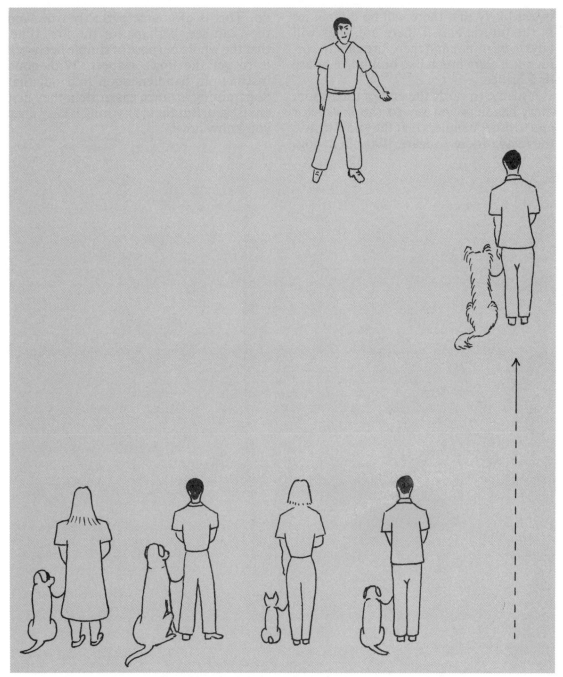

Fig. 10. When giving individual tuition in heelwork, it is best for the instructor to be on the left side of the handler and dog, and walking backwards so as to be able to talk to the rest of the class.

is less likely that there will be difficulties in the future; and if there are, they will tend to be minor and therefore easy to correct. It is very much like building a house or a bridge.

Usually, towards the end of the lesson, most handlers will say to the instructor and to other handlers that they now realise they have more to learn than their dogs do. This is of course perfectly true, and they can see, perhaps for the first time, that the whole purpose of simple heelwork is to get the dog's respect. With good instruction, handlers soon find out that dog training is much easier than they first envisaged. But then, anything is easy once you know how!

5

questions, answers and advice

After the practical work has finished an instructor should allocate enough time towards the end of the training period to answer the handlers' numerous and varied questions, and to give them advice with regard to their homework with their dogs during the forthcoming week.

It is a good idea at the end of a lesson for the handlers to be invited to assemble in a semicircle around the instructor and to be given a very brief *résumé* of what they have done during the lesson. The instructor should also express pleasure to the class on what they have just achieved. The praise gives a great boost to the handlers, especially the beginners.

When inviting questions, the instructor should first ask for those that apply to what the handlers have just learnt. When these have been answered, they may like to ask other questions, perhaps in regard to problems they are having with their dogs at home.

It is always advisable for the instructor to repeat a question, in a concise form if possible, so that if any of the handlers were not able to hear it in the first place, they can do so now.

One of the most common questions is: 'You said that it doesn't matter if a dog has an occasional sniff at something while you are walking freely, but that he must not sniff at all when he is heeling. How will the dog know when he is allowed to have the occasional sniff and when he's not?'

Now to some people the answer to that question is obvious. But a person asking a question should never be made to feel stupid, so the instructor can reply like this:

'Well, that's a very good question and one that many people ask. The answer is that when you say "Heel!" your dog is on duty and is not allowed to sniff until you dismiss it by saying "Go free". As soon as you say "Go free" he is then off duty and allowed to have the occasional sniff. Provided you are consistent in checking him if he sniffs when heeling, I can assure you that your dog will soon learn when he can and when he mustn't sniff.'

I guess it is understandable that some handlers cannot imagine that their dogs would ever be capable of learning anything; but when they see that they are, they just cannot believe their eyes. In fact they become overwhelmed and think that it's absolutely marvellous. The instructor's job here is to assure the handler that, given time, the dog will very quickly learn the difference between walking freely and heeling—and many more things as well.

There are usually quite a few questions about heelwork. When these have been answered, the instructor can call for questions that may refer to problems with the dogs in the home. A handler may ask: 'What can I do to stop my dog jumping up on visitors when they come to the front door? On top of that, he runs out the front door and into the street and won't come back when called. He returns home when it suits him.' The best way to answer that is to say something like this:

'Well, it's really quite easy. Firstly, as soon as you hear a knock at the front door, put your dog on the leash and take it with you to the door. That's just a basic principle and your leash and slip-collar are your equipment of control. When you open the door and your visitor steps inside, use your four-point principle: give the dog the *Command* "Get off", carry out your *Action* of jerking it down away from the visitor, and, as soon as you see the dog *Respond* by remaining on the ground, *Praise* it quietly. Use the same principle to correct it if it tries to run out of the house; and be sure to shut the door if the dog is off the leash. See how simple it is?'

There will be other questions pertaining to exercises the instructor has not yet covered. When these are asked it is best to reply by saying:

'Well, that would take me too long to cover now, and I'd rather deal with it in a future lesson when we have reached that aspect of the work. I can assure you that everything will be covered step by step in a very simple way.'

Having answered all the questions, the instructor should give the handlers advice on what they should do during the coming week:

'Handlers, during this next week, I would like you all to do a little bit of training every day, so that you don't forget what you have learnt today, and I am sure that your dogs will learn well and be ready for the next exercises I'll show you next week. If you happen to go out with your dog for about half an hour, free-walk it on the leash for about twenty minutes, and for the other ten minutes, which you can split up into two lots of five minutes, you can give your dog some simple heelwork. The best place to do it is on a long straight stretch of footpath, which should help to keep you walking straight. Select different roads that are fairly quiet and free of too many distractions. Think carefully before you do anything, prepare well, use your voice well, and use your hands and leash accurately. Always remember that you bring your dog to the training club to learn how to do the exercises, not just to train once a week. You must practise in your own locality. And please do not train your dog in the backyard. Let that be its play area. Dogs that are trained in their backyards will either perform well there but not at other places, or become utterly bored with training and refuse to do anything. So get them out to different areas to make it interesting and enjoyable for them. If you want to free-run your dog in a safe park and it will come back to you, then do so. But if it does not, don't take the risk.

'Well, that will be all for today, everyone. I thank you for your attention, the interest you have shown and the great efforts you have made. You have all done very well and I hope that you have enjoyed it as much as I have. I look forward to seeing you next week, when I'll show you how to do the turns in heelwork.'

It is most rewarding when you see handlers depart with smiles on their faces, having learnt that dog training is not as hard as they thought. They all have something to work towards now, and what seemed to be a chore in taking the dog out every day suddenly promises to be a pleasure.

6

how to conduct a class

I explained in Chapter 3 that by having the class standing in a line abreast of each other, the instructor was able to demonstrate heelwork in a straight line across in front of the class so that each handler could see from the side view where the dog was supposed to be, how it was to be corrected for surging forward and how it was taught to sit.

When it came to doing the practical work, I described in Chapter 4 how each handler under instruction heeled his or her dog forward in a straight line, correcting it if and when necessary, and then brought it to the sit position. So right from the first lesson all the handlers were made conscious of walking in straight lines. As you read on, you will understand why this is so important.

As I mentioned earlier, when I first started training at a dog club the handlers had to walk around one behind the other in a large circle whilst the instructor stood in the middle and shouted out the orders and tried to keep an eye on every handler. The handlers did the best they could, at times with great difficulties because they all had to keep moving at a constant speed until told to halt.

Then after a few years it was realised that when handlers walked around in a circle anticlockwise with the dogs on the inside, they were in fact walking into their dogs. The dogs, especially the highly sensitive ones, became afraid of being trodden on by their handlers and walked wide of them, sometimes lagging behind. Could one blame them? Some smart dogs, knowing that in a few seconds' time they would be further round the circle, kept trying to cut across it. Naturally their handlers kept jerking them into their left sides, but as this went on and on the poor dogs were receiving far too many jerks. It was not so bad when the instructor ordered the handlers to about-turn, so that they were then walking clockwise with the dogs on the outside; but the handlers were still not being made conscious of the importance of walking in a straight line.

In addition, many a dog tried to pull after the dog in front to sniff its rear, and in some cases dogs with aggressive tendencies tried to lunge and bite the dogs in front of them, often by grabbing their tails (if they had any). Sometimes these aggressive dogs would quickly turn and attempt to attack the dogs behind them. Many of the timid dogs became quite concerned about the dogs behind them, which made it most difficult for them to concentrate on heelwork and equally difficult for their handlers to train them to walk at heel.

In an all-breeds dog-training club, in which there can be dogs of many shapes and sizes, the dogs are not all going to be able to walk naturally at the same speed. Look at the natural walking speed of a Great Dane compared with that of a Corgi. Coupled with this is the difference in the walking speeds of the handlers.

There will be old and young people, tall and short, fit and not so fit. A tall, young and fit handler will feel comfortable walking fairly quickly, whereas a short, elderly handler, possibly suffering from something like arthritis, simply cannot match that speed.

The instructor standing in the centre of the circle also has difficulties. It is impossible to see the whole class at any one time, and when it is necessary to halt the class in

instructor

Fig. 11. Training in circles can create many difficulties. In this case (as they go round anticlockwise) handlers are walking into their dogs, the dogs are walking wide, some dogs pull after the ones in front, some become aggressive, and some lag. The instructor in the centre cannot see the whole class at any one time, and the handlers have difficulty in hearing the instructions.

order to explain something, the instructor would have the back turned on several of the handlers. Some instructors explain things by continuously turning around in the centre, so that everyone hears something; but just hearing fragments is no good at all. It is not quite so bad in a small hall with a small class, provided the acoustics are good; but outside, especially when it's windy, it is useless **(Fig. 11)**. If the instructor is on the outside of a circular class going around in a clockwise direction, he or she can at least see the whole class all the time. If there is any wind its direction should be noted, by throwing up a piece of grass into the air, and the instructor should then stand with the back to the wind so that the voice will be blown towards the class **(Fig. 12)**.

Classes working in circles sometimes tend to shift and encroach on adjacent classes, which can be a bit awkward. Also,

instructor   wind direction

Fig. 12.   Not so many problems occur when a class walks round clockwise. By standing on the outside with wind coming from behind, the instructor can see the whole class and can be heard by all the handlers.

the circle can keep getting larger or smaller, and when it gets smaller the dogs will be walking too close to each other and problems can arise.

Because of all this it was eventually decided to train handlers and dogs to walk in straight lines. Not only is every handler then learning to walk straight right from the first lesson, but no dog has another dog in front of it or behind it. Furthermore, if any handlers need to stop to correct their dogs, they can do so without getting in each other's way.

It is such a simple technique. Errors can be prevented, corrections can be made, good training can be taught to both handlers and dogs and the instructor can see the whole class all the time.

Sometimes when I explain these points in lectures, particularly in special courses for instructors, a young instructor will raise an objection that goes something like this: 'That's all very well for you—you've only got one person to train at a time. We've got large classes of anything up to twenty or more. We can't do that!' 'Why not?' I retort, knowing exactly what the answer will be. 'Well, you might start the class off in a straight line abreast of each other, but within a short time when you halt them they will be scattered all over the training area, because they all walk at different speeds. It won't work.'

I am always rather amused when I hear such comments, which have a negative flavour. So I immediately explain to that person and to the whole group how easy it is to keep control of a class in that respect. All you have to say to a class, as they stand in a line abreast of each other, is this:

'Handlers, when I give the command "Class, forward", I'm aware that you will all have your own speeds of walking, and some of you may have to stop from time to time to correct your

dogs. Now when I want you to come to a halt and sit your dogs, I won't suddenly yell out "Halt!". Instead I'll say "In line with your leader, handlers halt!". Whoever happens to be out in front is the leader at that particular time. So as soon as I give that order I want the leader to carefully *prepare* to sit his or her dog within the next few steps. As you each come up in line with the leader, you do the same and sit your dog, and *praise*. By doing it this way, the class will always keep together. There is another great advantage to this system: it gives me, as your instructor, a perfect opportunity of seeing most of you prepare and sit your dogs one after the other as you arrive in line with your leader. I can therefore give you individual tuition, if I think you need it. Just imagine what it would be like if I suddenly just yelled out "Halt!". I couldn't possibly watch you all sit your dogs so I wouldn't be able to help you, and furthermore you'd be scattered all over the training ground. I also know that if you did not prepare well, you'd more than likely make lots of mistakes in trying to sit your dogs the moment I yelled out "Halt!".'

After a while an observant instructor will get to know the difficulties and errors of individual handlers when sitting their dogs. So let us now imagine that I have a class of handlers walking along towards me. I am, of course, walking backwards. I see that Fred is out in front. I position myself near to him and say to the scattered class walking in their own straight lines, 'In line with your leader, handlers halt!':

'Now prepare well, Fred; sit your dog now, that's good. Praise your dog. Jean, come straight towards me. Keep your feet straight as you sit your dog. Good. Bert, keep the leash at 90° above his head, don't pull backwards. That's much better. Helen, bend at your knees as you sit your dog. Great! Jim, turn your left hand with your thumb facing to the left. That's right. Much easier, wasn't it? Ann, give your command "Sit" before you push down, not afterwards. Good. Susan, give a very quick sharp command to sit, repeat after me, "SIT!". Good, that was much better. Barbara, give your dog only one command to sit, not three or four. John, stroke your dog gently and slowly to keep it calm. If you ruffle it up, it will get all excited.'

So you can see how easy it is for an instructor to control a class with absolute ease and give individual tuition at the same time.

It is of course much easier if one is taking an obedience class in a breed club— a class of Old English Sheepdogs, for example: they are all about the same size, though their handlers might walk at slightly different speeds. When I was instructing in the RAF Police, the dogs were all German Shepherds, we all marched at the same speed, and there were no difficulties.

There are still a number of clubs today that continue to use the old system of heeling in circles. Some of them heel around so many times that after a while both handlers and dogs become bored stiff with the whole thing. Is it any wonder that they don't wish to attend any more?

Why have these clubs been reluctant to change? From what I have seen, there are various reasons. Some cannot see why they should change. Some do not realise what errors and difficulties they are creating for instructors, handlers and dogs. Some resist change because they appear to be governed by a hierarchy of the 'old school'. Such stubbornness is a pity, when they could so easily change and reap the benefits—or at least try out newer methods.

Surprisingly, some clubs have adopted the system of straight-line training in all but the beginner classes. I really cannot understand this. The whole point is that this is where the training starts and handlers need to have the right start and be taught to walk straight from the very first class.

I would never train classes in circles again—I don't want to go backwards. I want to go forwards, and like many trainers and instructors I am always looking for new and improved methods of training handlers and dogs. The more methods you have at your disposal the better it is. I have sometimes used a particular method in training a certain dog. Then a period of about ten years has elapsed before I have had to use the same method on another dog. You just never know when you might have to use some special technique. All dogs are different, and so are their handlers. You will also find that instructors are quite different. Some are extremely good, others are quite good and will obviously get better with experience, but unfortunately some just don't possess the qualities required.

I shall never forget the day I was invited to a dog-training club in Victoria in 1967. I had been in Australia for about three weeks. Soon after viewing the club I was asked if I would like to take some classes, which I was pleased to do. Everything went well with the first two classes that I took, but when I turned up the third time the head trainer told me he was short of instructors that day, so could I possibly take Classes II and III together—a total of about two dozen dogs and handlers. I agreed. 'Well, I'll leave you to it,' he said. 'But let me give you some advice. Don't stand any nonsense from these Australians!' For a moment I could not understand what he was getting at, for I knew that he was a born and bred Australian himself. So I asked him what he meant. 'Exactly what I say,' he retorted. 'Don't stand any nonsense from them! You've just come out from England where people are quite different with dogs. These Australians are tougher and you really have to be hard on 'em.' I was puzzled. 'But I haven't experienced any trouble with them,' I protested. 'On the contrary, I have found everyone most appreciative and cooperative.' To which he responded, 'Well, this is how I drill 'em: I get 'em all lined up and say, "Forward! Right turn! Left turn! Right-about turn! Halt! Come on, hurry up, get a grip of your dog. Forward!" And so on, that's how I do it.' I looked at him in astonishment, and asked, 'Were you in the army?' 'Yes!' he replied. 'I thought so,' I said. 'Well I'm sorry, but I'm not going to talk to these nice people like that. They are civilians and they've all come here of their own free will to learn how to train their pet dogs, and I am only too happy to train them. And I cannot see any difference between training here and training in England.' 'Have it your own way,' he replied in annoyance and walked off.

I took the class, everything went extremely well and I was very pleased. But I did not return to that club again.

7

turns in heelwork

Once handlers have grasped the idea of the general procedure of heelwork, the next thing they need to know is how to do the turns.

The instructor should explain very briefly that turns in obedience dog training have two purposes. Firstly, they take you to where you want to go, which is quite obvious; secondly (and more importantly), they enable you to gain even more respect from your dog.

It is best for the instructor to face across the front of the class when giving the demonstration.

right-about turn

'The first turn that I am going to show you today is the right-about turn. Up until now you have been holding the handle of the leash plus one other point further down the leash, all in your right hand. You will notice that there are three pieces of leash hanging down from your right hand. If you now take those three pieces in one grasp with your left hand, and remove your right hand from the two loops it was holding, you will have your right hand perfectly free to pat your right leg at the same height above the ground as your dog's neck. The sound made when you slap your leg a few times as you say in a very interesting tone "Sam, heel!" should attract the dog to come around as you pick your feet up and turn around on the spot. As soon as you see its

head respond to come around, praise it vocally. Once you have turned around continue walking in a straight line along the line you were walking prior to the right-about turn. As you walk, all that remains to be done is to put your right hand back through the two loops of leash, then let go with your left hand, and you're back to where you started.

'Now I said that your dog *should* respond: there is always the possibility that it will not, especially if it is distracted just at the moment when you are doing the turn. If this happens don't worry, because you have already taken hold of the leash in your left hand in one grasp—whereby there should exist about 30 cm (1 ft) of leash between your left hand and the clip of your leash —and if you keep your left hand down on your left knee (at the same height above the ground as the dog's neck), you are then in the ideal position to give the dog a short, sharp, horizontal jerk in the direction you wish to go if it does not instantly obey your command. If, and only if, you have to give such jerks to uphold your command, always ensure that your left hand returns instantly to your left knee, so that the 30 cm of leash hangs in a U-shape once again. Now as I see it, most of you will have to keep both hands down to your knees, but Lillian, since you have a Great Dane you'll need to keep your hands at waist height; and Nancy, because you have an Australian Terrier you'll need to bend down and keep your hands at ankle height. So always remember to keep your hands down to the height of the dog you are training.

Now watch as I walk across in front of you with Sam at heel. I've decided to do a right-about turn. I have the dog's attention. I now prepare by taking the leash in my left hand, let go with the right, keep both hands down to the dog's height, pat my leg, and say "Sam, heel!". He responds. I say "Good dog", and now I come back putting my right hand into these two loops and let go with my left. Watch again, I'll do it twice more.'

It is important for the instructor to give a running commentary with this demonstration so that handlers can hear, see and understand everything.

When it comes to doing the practical work with the class, it is a good idea for the instructor to get the handlers to practise the correct way of transferring the leash from one hand to the other and back again before they do anything with their dogs. It is time well spent, because if they don't do it correctly they may well lose control of the dog. It also makes them much more conscious, right from the start, that they should always know how to hold a leash in the exercises they are teaching the dog.

Having done this, which everyone finds very easy, I would then make it equally easy for them to do the actual turn, by saying:

'Handlers, I would like you to imagine that you are walking along as you do this first right-about turn on the spot where you are standing. Take hold of the leash in your left hand, remove your right hand, put *both* your hands down to your dog's height (imagine you're still walking along). Now when I say "Right-about turn" pat your right leg, say your dog's name and "Heel" as you pick your feet up to turn around, and then proceed forward, putting your right hand back into the two loops. After a few steps, sit your dog. Ready? Right-about turn!'

Most people learn this best by doing it from a stationary position first. They can

do it once or twice like this before trying it while actually walking along, and the results are usually most encouraging.

Before each right-about turn, the instructor should prepare the handlers well by telling them what to do:

'I want you to get ready for a right-about turn. Put the leash into your left hand, remove your right hand, keep both hands down. Right-about turn. Say "Heel!" and praise "Good dog!". Now put your right hand back into the two loops.'

When saying 'Right-about turn', the instructor can slap the leg a few times so that the handlers can hear. This reminds them what to do without having to be told —a very useful technique. The instructor can also split the class, so that while one half does the turn the other half can watch; then they can swap over. This gives everyone the opportunity of seeing it done a few times as well as actually doing it.

right turn

'Well, I think that you all learnt that right-about turn very well. That was very good. Now I'll show you how to do the right turn, which needs very little explanation and demonstration. The procedure is exactly the same as for the right-about turn. The main difference is that it is only half the angle, 90° instead of 180°. However, in order to get the best attention from your dogs I would like you to watch carefully how I use my feet as I demonstrate in a small square in front of you. I shall start off by walking towards you and I'll do the first right turn when I get within two to three metres of you. When I pat my leg, say "Sam, heel!" and turn sharply on my feet, the dog will suddenly see me change direction and will go with me to the right. If I turned right by gradually walking round in a quarter of a circle I would not be capturing Sam's full attention. So watch in particular my footwork as I do just four right turns in a square, and observe also the reaction of the dog.'

Having given the demonstration it is always a good idea to say something like this:

'Well, there you are, handlers, you can see how easy it is. I'm sure you're all keen to have a go, aren't you? Well, in order to give you all some individual tuition, you will notice that I've set out four flags forming a square, and I would like to have eight of you out there in position, spaced out equally, two to a side. I would like the rest of the class to watch. I shall place myself at this corner so that as you each come straight towards me I can give you individual attention. You can then practise your right turns on the other three corners yourselves. I have chosen this corner because from here the wind today will carry my voice across to all eight of you and to those watching on the far side. I shall extend my left arm and foot in the direction I want you to turn.' **(Fig. 13)**

This way of teaching large classes to do right turns, and later left turns, is very efficient. Maximum results can be gained with a minimum of effort. The instructor, who remains in one place, can give individual tuition to each handler, and that's the most important thing. The 'audience' learns by watching as their dogs are relaxing. When the handlers have gone round once, the instructor will spot their particular difficulties or faults and, as they come round the second time, will know exactly what to tell them. For instance:

'As you come to me, Fred, keep *both* your hands down. Good, that's better. Lillian, come straight towards me and turn sharply, don't round the corner off. Excellent! Jim, keep your left hand straight down, keep a slack lead. Yes, that's much better. Helen, pat your leg before you turn, not afterwards. Good, you've got it! John, use a more interesting voice when you say the dog's name and "Heel". Nancy, don't go round too quickly, aim straight at me, then turn; now proceed. Ann, you're doing everything well, but don't forget to praise as your dog responds.

That's better, now practise it on the other corners. Geoff, give your dog a quick little jerk if it doesn't respond to your command. Yes, that's good, well timed.'

When they have gone round the third time they will be much better, and on the fourth time they will be very good. The instructor has an unimpeded view of handlers doing the turn on the corner diagonally opposite, and should praise when a good turn is seen on that corner.

Four laps round the square should be sufficient, after which that group can swap places with the audience. The second group often learns more quickly than the first, because it has had the advantage of watching. If at any time the instructor feels it necessary to emphasise any general points, it is best to halt the class for that purpose before they go round again.

If the class consists of dogs of various heights, it is a good idea to split it by putting all the small dogs in one group and all the large dogs in the other. This can prevent a little Maltese Terrier, say, from holding up a big Irish Wolfhound.

left turn

After the second group has done the right turns it can turn inward and relax while the left turn is briefly explained and demonstrated within the square.

'Handlers, I shall now show you how to do the left turn, which is very easy. You don't have to transfer the leash from one hand to the other—you carry it quite normally in your right hand all the time. When you want to turn left, take hold of the clip part of the leash with your left hand with thumb on the top, say "Heel!" quickly and give a quick horizontal jerk back, enough to stop the dog proceeding any further forward. In that fraction of a second, spin on the ball of your left foot to the left and the dog, seeing your right foot come round, will automatically turn its head to

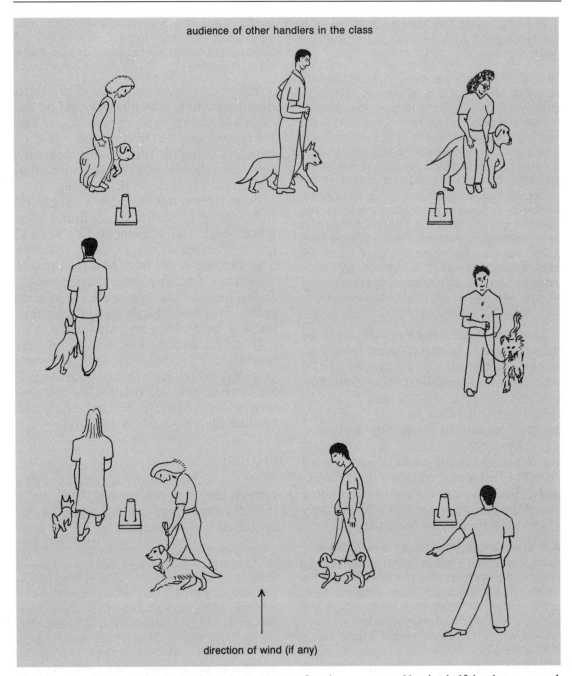

audience of other handlers in the class

direction of wind (if any)

Fig. 13.   The right turn. By placing four witches' hats or flags in a square and having half the class go round, the instructor can stand at one corner and give individual tuition to each handler. The wind direction should be noted, so that all the handlers, including those watching on the far side, can hear.

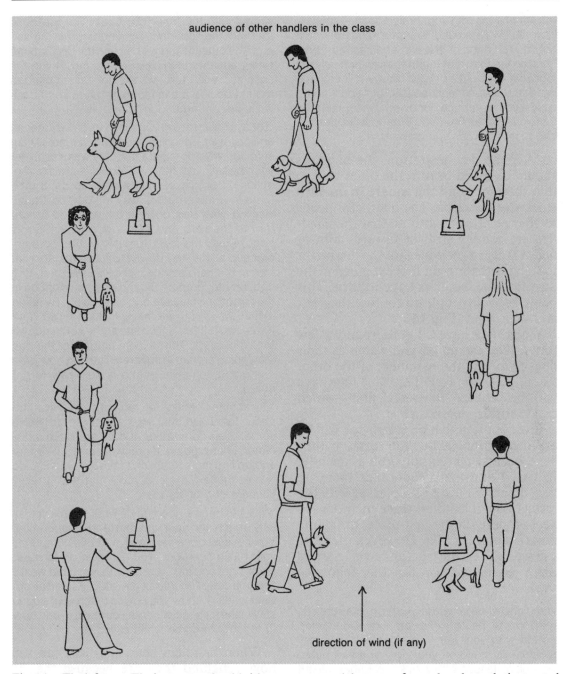

audience of other handlers in the class

direction of wind (if any)

Fig. 14.   The left turn. The instructor should either move around the corner from where he or she instructed the right turn, or move to the adjacent corner, so that the handlers are going straight towards their instructor.

the left and go with you. Praise upon response. Now, as I walk around in a small square watch only my left hand on the first and second turns. Then on the third and fourth turns watch only my footwork. I know it's difficult for you to watch the hand and feet simultaneously, but you'll find it easy if you watch the handwork twice, then the footwork twice. Then you'll be able to put the two together when you come to do it.'

After the demonstration, the handlers should be asked to turn the other way so that they go round the square in an anticlockwise direction. The instructor needs to alter position slightly so that the handlers are coming straight towards him or her. It is also a good idea for the instructor to stand with the right foot extended in the direction the handlers have to turn. This helps, as some people do confuse their left and their right **(Fig. 14)**.

When they have all gone round a few times, they can go off and watch as their dogs relax and the members of the other team take their place. This time *they* have had the chance to watch first—which makes it fair, doesn't it?

It is not often that an instructor will be asked questions about the turns, if they have been taught simply and efficiently. In fact, I find that people pick them up very quickly and are very pleased with the results. And if handlers teach their dogs to heel properly in the first place, doing the turns is a piece of cake. However, there are a few points the instructor needs to stress when giving advice for the following week:

'Handlers, when you do left turns, make sure you spin on the ball of your left foot. Don't step around with your left foot otherwise you may accidentally tread on your dog's paw or bump the side of its face with your knee. Either will put the dog off.'

'Perhaps you will have noticed that we didn't use the dog's name with the left turn, whereas we did with the other two turns. The reason is that with the right-about and right turns, the dog is on the outside and we can use the dog's name to our advantage in calling it around. But in the case of the left turn, we are not calling the dog around us. We are in fact telling it to keep back while we get around in front of it.

'Today I have shown you these turns in rather an artificial way, by going around in squares. I am sure you will appreciate that this was mainly for your benefit, so that you could learn by repetition. Now that you know what to do, try the turns in a more natural way in your local area. Heeling your dog down a footpath, do a right turn to the kerb and sit the dog at the kerb's edge. Cross the road, turn left on the footpath, proceed a little way down the footpath, do a left turn to the kerb's edge, sit, cross the road, turn right on the footpath and proceed straight on in the direction you were originally going. By doing it that way, you will have included two right turns, two left turns, two sits at the kerb and two road crossings. This is more natural for the dog than going around in squares. The dog now feels it is going somewhere and is not likely to get bored.

'On another section of footpath do two right-about turns. Do one, walk about ten or twelve steps, then do another. If they are quite satisfactory, keep going. If not, walk on a bit further and do two more. It doesn't take a moment to do two of these turns and you'll find that it really keeps a dog on its toes.

'Well, it's been a good day's work. Thank you all very much for your interest and cooperation. You have all done very well, and this completes your basic heelwork. You can now go forward, back, right and left (north, south, east and west), and you can of course sit your dog. Keep it all up. Next week I'll show you how to teach your dog to stay in the sit position while you leave it, and how to teach it to come when called.'

When handlers hear this, you can see how delighted they are because that is what they really want to be able to do with their dogs. It makes them look forward eagerly to the next lesson.

8

the recall and the sit-stay

I always feel that the nicest and most polite way of starting off subsequent lessons is to welcome all the handlers and ask them how they have been getting on during the past week. Then I tell them that we will spend about ten minutes going over the basic heelwork, to ensure that everything is in place, before moving on to the first stages of the sit-stay and training their dogs to come.

A simple way to assemble a scattered class into one straight line is for the instructor to stretch out both arms and say:

'Would you all like to line up abreast of each other facing me please. Ann, you stand there facing me; now if the rest of you could take up your positions each side of Ann, leaving a good space between you and your neighbour's dog. That's good. Thank you. Before we start, I would like to see that you all have your training slip-collars on the correct way. I won't come up to every dog and inspect every collar—that takes time, and some of the more timid dogs might feel threatened. Instead, I'll walk across in front of the class from the right-hand end, about two metres away from you all, and if you would each put your left hand behind and just a little way through the collar, and pull the leash gently with

your right hand, I'll be able to see that the collars are on correctly. Thank you.'

Instructors should carry out this inspection before they start the actual lesson. If it is done this way, it can be over in a matter of seconds.

The revision in heelwork should not be for very long. Two or three right-about turns and two or three sits, followed by a few right turns and left turns around in a square formed by four flags or red cones (commonly called witches' hats), will be quite sufficient. Afterwards, the instructor should congratulate the class on their good work.

Now I don't think it really matters which of the next two exercises dogs learn first—the recall or the sit-stay. But if limited for time I would always opt for the recall first, because that is the most important exercise in all forms of dog training.

recall

Have you ever thought how many people would wonder what you were talking about if you asked, 'Can your dog do a recall?' Well, I'll never forget being asked this question when I first joined a dog-training club. The word 'recall' puzzled me at first. I had only ever heard the noun in the cinema Westerns: the US cavalry would be pursuing the Indians on horseback, the Captain would order, 'Bugler, sound the Recall!' and the cavalry would return. So I thought quickly, 'What's all this? I don't have a bugle and my dog has never heard one!' I had to ask, 'What do you mean?' I always have a little laugh when I reminisce about those days.

Before giving a brief explanation of the recall exercise, I would make sure that the handlers and dogs were relaxed; that the wind, if any, was coming more or less from behind me; and that the handlers were not being blinded by the sun, which might be shining at a low angle. So instructors should note these things and position the class and themselves in the best way possible.

The introduction to the exercise should be made clearly and briefly:

'Handlers, today I am going to show you how to teach your dogs to come to you. We call this the recall, because we are recalling our dogs to us.

'Today Jock has very kindly lent me his dog, Mac, with whom I am going to demonstrate the recall. In a few moments I shall walk out there, turn around and, with the dog walking freely on the leash out in front of me, casually stroll towards you as you stand there in a group. When the dog nearly reaches you, I shall call him enthusiastically "Mac, come!" and immediately walk slowly backwards in a straight line. As the dog responds by turning around I shall praise him at once and after two to three steps backwards I shall take up just half of the leash into one hand, so that Mac doesn't get his feet tangled in the leash. Keeping both my hands between my knees I shall continue to talk to him and work him on the remaining half of the leash.

If for any reason he tries to divert to the left or to the right, I shall correct him by taking hold of the clip part of the leash with my spare hand (not the one already holding the leash in two places), say "Come!" and jerk him accurately and horizontally at his height to the centre of my body again, let go with my spare hand and praise "Good boy!". If he goes just past me, I shall stop, jerk him back to be in front of me again, and then repeat "Come, good boy!". Finally, when I consider he has done fairly well, I shall gather up all the leash into one hand, place my spare hand over his hindquarters as I am still walking slowly backwards, say "Sit!" and push down on his hindquarters towards me. Then I'll praise him, and finally dismiss him. So watch carefully as I do this. I shall do it twice and then you can all do it, one by one, with your own dogs.'

The same explanations can be repeated during the actual demonstration, so that handlers can see how it is done, how the corrections, if any, are made and how the correct intonation of voice should be given. Having eye-contact with the whole group as well as with the dog, the instructor is in the ideal position and can describe to the handlers what he or she is doing—e.g. praising the dog, keeping it calm and keeping its attention in the sit position. By allowing the dog to rest its bottom jaw in the hands, the instructor can give praise slowly and gently by stroking with thumbs only from the dog's eyes towards its ears; this has a calming effect. On no account should the dog be allowed to look around until it is dismissed. If it does look around while being praised, it will think the praise is for looking around; this will lead to further distraction. The instructor should show handlers how to correct a dog immediately if it should look around, by saying 'Leave' and either giving a short sharp upward jerk on the leash or taking hold of the dog by the scruff of its neck, both sides with both hands, and giving one quick little shake. The dog must be praised the instant it responds and looks towards the person training it.

I believe it is necessary to demonstrate this exercise twice, and a third time if requested. Handlers get the main idea when they see it for the first time, and on the second demonstration they can follow it in more detail. No time should then be lost in individual tuition. Each handler should do it at least twice and all the handlers should be encouraged to watch each time. So if there are a dozen in a class, each handler would have seen the recall done at least twenty-two times in that lesson—and will have learnt a lot by seeing it done repeatedly like that. It is up to the instructor to keep the class interested in every dog being trained.

When teaching this exercise, the best position for the instructor to adopt is walking alongside the handler towards the class. Not only can the handler be shown what to do; the whole class can observe particular points in the process of the recall **(Fig. 15)**. If the instructor had the back to the class, they would feel they were being ignored and would find it hard to hear the instructions. I have seen this happen hundreds of times in obedience classes and after a while the handlers won't even bother to watch; they pass the time by nattering to each other.

One of the worst mistakes an instructor can make in teaching this exercise is to tell the handlers to run backwards when calling their dogs. If they do, they will more than likely excite their dogs, which could make them jump up, get their legs caught in the leashes, run past the handlers or become generally distracted. It can also be very dangerous. The handlers could slip or topple backwards if their dogs jumped at them, and we cannot afford to have un-

necessary accidents. When instructors tell people to run backwards it is usually to teach their dogs to come quickly. Yet the most important thing at this early stage is to teach the handlers and dogs what to do, and how to do it with accuracy. Walking backwards slowly keeps the dogs calm and helps the handlers keep their balance better. It also gives them more time to think about what they are doing so that they can do it correctly. Speed in the recall will come later, when the dogs are much further away, and I will come to that. At this stage, accurancy is the key word.

When it comes to question time with this important exercise the questions can be quite numerous. Most of them can be answered during the practical work as the faults and problems occur. One question often asked is, 'What happens if my dog does not respond when I first call him?' The answer is: 'Give the dog a jerk towards you on the full length of the leash, horizontally at the dog's height. This jerk is to uphold your command, just as you would use it in other exercises.' Another question is, 'What do I do if my dog mouths my hands?' The answer is the same as for any other time that it does so: 'Take hold, say "No!" and give it a quick shake.' Never allow your dog to mouth you, your clothing or the leash. It is an expression of the dog wanting its own way.

Handlers will often say that when their dogs have been called and are sitting in front of them, they don't like receiving the physical praise and try to twist around and pull away. I can well understand handlers thinking this, but I point out that it isn't a case of not liking the physical praise; rather it's a case of wanting their own way, wanting to look around at other things. As soon as that distraction is corrected and

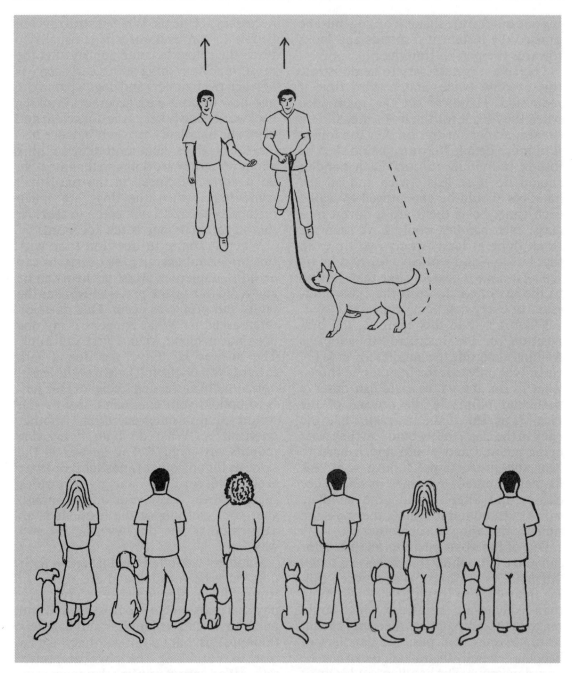

Fig. 15.   The recall while free-walking. It is best for the instructor to walk alongside the handler as they go towards the class. Not only can the handler be shown what to do; the whole class can observe particular points as the dog is recalled and handler and instructor walk backwards.

full attention is gained, the dogs will lap up the vocal and physical praise.

Perhaps the best advice an instructor can give to a class for practising this exercise during the coming week is to try it when free-walking along a footpath. If the dog happens to see a stray dog, this is an ideal time to call your dog in order to get its total respect: when it is called, it must come under all circumstances. But a little word of warning: handlers should make sure that no-one is walking behind them when they call their dogs!

sit-stay

When giving a brief explanation of the sit-stay exercise, all the instructor needs to say is something like this: 'Handlers, now that you all know how to sit your dogs, we will go further by teaching them to stay in that sitting position while we leave them to go out in front of them, and after a few seconds return to their right sides again.' That's all; further instructions as to how to do it can be given when demonstrating with a dog:

'As you see, Janice has kindly lent me her dog Cloe, so that I can demonstrate this exercise. In a few moments I shall get Cloe to sit beside me. I'll hold the leash in my left hand vertically above her head, say "Stay" and step slowly in front of her at one straight arm's length away. If she moves at any time I shall quickly say "Sit", give her a little jerk upwards and relax the leash again. If she gets up completely and tries to take off, I shall immediately take her back to the same spot by saying "Heel!", then "Sit!", then "Stay!" and start all over again. If a dog is not taken back to the very same spot and facing the same way, but is told to sit, say, a few steps beyond the original position, it will have gained that much ground and, having discovered this, will get up again and again. So whenever a stay is being taught, it is essential that the handler make a mental note of the exact spot where the dog was told to stay. Now watch carefully as I sit her beside me facing away from the class.'

Taking up this position, an instructor can turn his head around to the left so that the class can hear.

'Stay! I now step slowly around through 180° to face the front of the dog, by moving my right foot first, twisting slowly on my left toe, and stepping back a little. You can see that I am now a straight arm's length away and facing the dog (Fig. 16). I have the word "Sit" on the tip of my tongue should the dog attempt to get up, and my left hand is poised vertically above her head in order to give a little jerk upwards to uphold my command. You will also notice that the leash is still just slack. I shall now move around slowly in a frontal semicircle, which enables me to keep my left hand above the dog's head. Having stepped round to the left and right and returned to being in front of her again, I shall now return to my original position beside her, wait a few seconds, praise her, and then dismiss her.'

This is a very easy exercise to explain and demonstrate because it is a stationary one, and it is based on what the dog has learnt in the first lesson—namely, to sit. But before the practical work is carried out by the class, it can be a good idea for the instructor to ask a question which should not be too hard even for beginners to answer: 'You would have heard that when I told the dog to stay I said "Stay!" not "Cloe, stay!". Why do you think I omitted her name?' After a few seconds someone will usually offer an answer in an enquiring way: 'Well, is it because the dog might have moved if you had used her name?' 'Yes, you're right. But why do you think that would have been so?' Someone else will answer more positively: 'Because you'd already used the dog's name with "Heel" and she would associate that with moving off with you.' 'Yes, that's well explained, and now I can see how you are

Fig. 16. The sit-stay. When demonstrating the first stage of this exercise it is best for the instructor to face the dog and the class. The owner of the dog can stand close by.

all beginning to think like dogs! That's great. It means you're starting to develop a deeper understanding of how a dog's mind works.'

It is always a good idea to do the practical work for the first time with half the class, while the other half watches. A very easy way to organise this when they are all in a long straight line is to ask them to number themselves from the right. The first person at the end says 'One!', the second says 'Two!' and so on all the way down the line, so that they all know their numbers. Then the instructor can say, 'Odd numbers only, forward with your dogs ten paces and sit your dogs.' The rest of the class (the even numbers) can be asked to watch. The instructor should then ensure that all the handlers are prepared by having their leashes in their left

hands vertically above their dogs' heads. The leashes should be just slack. The amount of leash showing will vary with the height of the dog and the height of the handler's hand when stretched out horizontally above its head.

'When I say "Leave your dogs", I want you to say "Stay!". Say it firmly without shouting it, and say it only once. As soon as you have said it, step around slowly in front of your dogs.'

When the instructor says 'Leave your dogs' he or she should also say 'Stay!', so that the handlers will know immediately how to say the word: 'Are you ready? Leave your dogs! Stay!' Everyone then echoes the instructor's voice with 'Stay!'. It is important that the instructor keep reminding the handlers to watch their own dogs very intently and keep their left hands in the same position above the dogs' heads with leashes just slack. The instructor should also keep the interest of the other half of the class by asking them to observe carefully.

'Now would you like to return to your dogs by the same way you left them? Stand quite still beside them for a few more seconds and continue to keep your eyes on them. They could still move even now, and if they do you must correct them immediately. Now very gently and very slowly and very quietly praise your dogs. "Good dog! Very good! There's a good dog!" Now you can dismiss them. Thank you very much, you have all done very well. Would you now change places with the rest of the class and watch them as they do the exercise.'

Once again it can be seen that if this instructional technique is used, all the handlers have the opportunity of watching as well as actually doing. It is also easier for the instructor to instruct and watch only half of the class at a time. The dogs are being trained only half the time, whereas all the handlers are learning all the time!

At question time, one of the questions asked at about this stage in training is: 'When do you, or when should you, use the dog's name with a command?— because I feel that I'll never be able to remember when to use my dog's name and when not to.'

'Yes, that's a good question and one that puzzles many people. A very simple rule to remember is that with all stationary exercises like the sit, stand and drop, or the stay in any of those three positions, you don't use the dog's name. With exercises involving movement, as in the recall, in going forward and in the right and right-about turn in heelwork, you can use your dog's name and should do so in the early days of training. You will also note that I did not include the left turn on that list, because when you teach

a left turn the dog is, for a fraction of a second, stationary when you give it a quick little jerk back. Interesting isn't it, when you analyse it all.'

Some general advice for handlers with the sit-stay exercise is that they can include it in their daily heelwork, apart from doing it as a separate exercise. And if it is pouring with rain, which prevents training outside, the sit-stay on the leash can always be taught indoors. Surprisingly a lot of people never think of that. There is always something you can do with your dog when the weather is bad.

Not so very long ago I took the opportunity of watching a certain class in an obedience club. It was obvious that one handler had difficulty in teaching his dog to stay off the leash. So the instructor called him out in front of the class, asked him to remove his leash, and told him to leave his dog and walk straight ahead for several metres. The handler said 'Stay!' and left his dog. After he had walked a few steps forward, the dog got up and followed him. The instructor told the handler that his dog had got up, whereupon the handler turned around, made the dog sit again in a new position, told him 'Stay!' and walked away again. The same thing happened. In fact it happened six times, by which time the dog was about 25 metres further on from the first spot. Finally the instructor said, 'Well, keep working on it at home.' You can imagine the handler's frustration, can't you? But was the dog at fault? No, not really, because he was not being trained properly. Was the handler at fault? No, not really, simply because he did not receive the correct instruction. You can see who was at fault, can't you? Yes, the instructor. Of course you could take that further and enquire who trained the instructor. But the main point is that if the correct instruction is not given, handlers will continuously make such mistakes and end up with problems.

The instructor should have told the handler (a) to keep his eyes on his dog, so that he could correct it the moment it moved, and (b) to take the dog back to the original spot, which could easily have been marked by placing something on the grass. Quite frankly I felt sorry for the instructor, the handler and the dog: all three had been trained incorrectly. I find it most annoying when I see such elementary mistakes being made. It is also most annoying for handlers when they find out that such faults could have been prevented if the correct instruction had been given in the first place.

9

the recall off the leash

After the instructor has welcomed every-one to the next lesson and asked generally how they are all getting on, a little time should be spent in revising what they have learnt to date. Only a little heelwork needs to be given, and perhaps two sit-stays can be included in that heelwork. Then the instructor should have a look at the recalls on the leash in free-walking.

'Well, that all seems to be going very well indeed, and from what I've just seen it's clear that you have all been working conscientiously and consistently. I can tell this by the way you are doing everything as individuals and also by the way your dogs are responding. As I mentioned in my preliminary lecture, I can always tell whether handlers have been practising during the week. Keep up the good work.

'Today I am going to show you how you can put two exercises together, which happens a lot in dog training. I am going to show you how to recall the dog from the sit-stay position. Joan has kindly lent me her dog Boz, with whom I will now demonstrate. I shall start off by getting him to sit at my side so that our backs are facing you. I'll now tell him "Stay!" and, holding only the handle of the leash in my left hand, I turn around to face him and all of you and move back a little with my left hand outstretched so that the leash is hanging in a loop between us. You will also be able to judge from where you are all standing that my thumbnail is in direct line with his eyes

and my eyes, which I'll open as wide as I can. It's amazing what you can do with your eyes. Isn't that good attention, everyone? We have eye-contact and he has the sight of my hand as well. Now I'll call him. Boz, come! Good boy! As you can see, as I walk back and gather in the leash he is responding perfectly. Now I'll get him to sit: Sit! And now the praise: Good boy!

'Well, I'm sure you'll all agree that Joan has obviously put in some good work with this dog during the past week. I shall now go one stage further, and before I say "Stay" I'll discreetly drop the leash, but I'll pretend that I have the leash in my left hand, which will be outstretched as before. Stay! Now that I'm out in front can you see him gazing up at me? Now watch. Boz, come! Good boy! Watch how I use my hands as I pretend to gather up an imaginary leash. He is following my hands as I talk to him, and now that he has come right up to me as I'm still walking slowly backwards, I take hold of the real leash near the clip and tell him "Sit!", and praise him gently and quietly for a while. Good boy, clever dog! To finish off, I shall stand beside him, heel him forwards a few paces, sit him, and then dismiss him. Boz, heel! Good boy!—Sit! Good boy! —Go free! Good boy!

'Well, that all went off very well, didn't it? You can see now how easy it is if you take it step by step and keep to the basic principles of training. But you may possibly be wondering why I finished off with the little piece of straight heelwork. The reason is this. It helps to maintain in the dog's mind the importance of coming in straight. In time dogs get to know the next part of an exercise. In this case, after the dog has done the recall he will expect to continue on in the same straight line. This method helps to establish that straight-line concept in the dog's mind and therefore makes him less likely to divert in the recall. If you learn this method now, you'll be able to use it with more advanced exercises later.'

It is then time for the instructor to get all the handlers to do the recall as just demonstrated. The first recall is by holding the leash; if that is satisfactory, the second recall can be done by dropping the leash (**Fig. 17**).

Now as a precaution and to give handlers confidence, it is a good idea for the instructor to attach a light, long line on each dog as it does the second recall—so that if any dog should suddenly run off, the handler can correct it vocally and the instructor physically with a jerk on the line. It is therefore best for the instructor to be standing about 2 to 3 metres to one side between the dog and the handler (**Fig. 18**).

If time permits the instructor can ask each handler to follow up these two short recalls from the sit-stay position by doing another while free-walking. As the handler and dog, strolling towards the class, get within about 20 metres, the instructor can say, 'Drop the leash out of your hand, walk backwards, call your dog.' This really makes the handler rely on the voice, and

Fig. 17. The recall from the sit-stay position. Having dropped the leash and said 'Stay', the handler turns around to face the dog with arm outstretched as if holding the leash. The dog should respond and recognise the handler's hand-movements when recalled.

the moment the dog responds the instructor should say to the handler: 'Praise your dog. Keep talking. Keep walking backwards and keep your hands together between your knees. Now take hold of the clip part of the leash, sit your dog and praise with your voice and hands.'

The funny thing I have noticed about this stage of doing the recall is that whenever I tell handlers to drop their leashes, they are reluctant to do so and I have to repeat my instruction a second and even a third time. And often, when their dogs respond, the handlers forget to praise and continue to use all their resources to ensure that the dog completes the exercise. That's why I continue to give them instructions, because I don't want anything to go wrong. The instructor has to communicate quickly using as few words as possible. It is not sufficient to give the order 'Call your dog!' just as you would hear a steward or a judge say it in the obedience trial ring. The instructor must be thinking ahead all the time, following up the initial orders with quick, brief instructions time and time again until it all becomes second nature to the handlers.

As an instructor I always get a thrill out of training when I see the dog come straight back to the handler on the initial command. When I see this I say something like, 'That's excellent. I'm sure you are very pleased with that, aren't you?' 'Pleased?' the handler exclaims. 'I'm ab-

Fig. 18.   If it is anticipated that a dog may run off in the recall, a light line can discreetly be attached to the dog and held by the instructor, who should stand to one side.

solutely astounded! I just never thought my dog would ever come to me. Before I came for training, he would always run away.'

I have noticed that in most obedience clubs the recall is always done from the sit-stay position. I think this is because they are preparing dogs for the trial ring. Many of the dogs are trained so well that they get full marks from the judge. But when some of those dogs are running free in a park somewhere, they will not come when called but will continue to sniff around and totally ignore their handlers. The reason is that the dogs have been taught to come only in a trial situation—and if you think about it, those dogs are already on duty then, as they've been told to stay in the sitting position. Well, there is not much point in training a dog to gain obedience titles if it won't come at other times. That is why I believe in doing many more recalls when the dog is walking free off the leash than from a sit-stay position. So I urge obedience clubs and their instructors to include this in their training programmes, and can assure them that

they and their handlers will greatly improve their training and reap the benefits.

During subsequent weeks the recall with most dogs can be perfected until they come instantly on command and sit automatically in front of their handlers. However, quite a few dogs do develop faults in the recall and if these are not corrected immediately they will persist and in some cases become worse. Some dogs are too slow; others are so fast that they knock their handlers over! There are dogs that are inattentive; others become habitual sniffers. Some sit away from the handlers; others sit in crooked lazy positions. A few dogs are stubborn and will not come at all; others walk off and will come only when it suits them. And so on. The instructors then have the extra task of showing the handlers how to correct such faults. You will find, however, that the vast majority of these faults have been allowed to continue from the early days of training. They could have been prevented in the first place.

10

footwork

Footwork is a very important aspect of dog training. When good footwork is used, excellent results are achieved; whereas bad footwork can cause many problems.

In basic heelwork I stressed the importance of walking in straight lines and of carrying out the three turns simply and accurately. If at any time handlers walk into their dogs while heeling, or step into them when teaching them to sit, the dogs will become wary of their handlers' feet and will, as a result, walk wide and sit wide.

crooked sits

Now even if handlers do walk straight, their dogs will sometimes sit crooked and possibly too far forward, and it is important that all handlers be shown how to correct these faults. An ideal time for this would be in about the third or fourth lesson. To explain and demonstrate how a crooked sit should be corrected, the instructor can say something like this:

'Handlers, you have all been doing very well with your dogs over the first few weeks, and up until now I have told you to pull your dogs in with your hands if at any time they have sat crooked, too far forward or in a floppy posture. That was all right to start with, but if you continue to do this your dogs will let you do all the work. So today

I'm going to show you how you can correct these faults by getting your dog up on its own four feet and teaching it to come close in to your left side to sit straight beside you. This is known as the correction of a crooked sit.

'Since you are in line abreast of each other, I shall stand in front of John, who is on the extreme right, so that my feet are facing the same way as his are. You will now be able to follow my footsteps. As you can see, Buffy, whom Margaret has kindly lent me, is sitting crooked, floppy and too far forward in relation to me.

'Before I do anything with the dog, I will explain the footwork. Keeping my right foot where it is, I cast my left well back in a curve behind my right, like this. Then I bring it forward again. Would you all like to try that? Cast the left foot well back in a curve; now bring it forward again. Try it once more. That's good! That's all you have to do with your feet.

'Now when I cast my left foot back in an arc, I shall hold the clip part of the leash in my left hand, and keep my left hand at the same height from the ground as the dog's neck. I shall invite the dog to heel and lead him around in the shape of a letter S in reverse. That means, I shall turn him in towards me, then back slightly away from me, and in towards me again. As he comes in towards my left foot, I shall take it forward. Buffy, thinking that I'm going to continue forward, will, I am sure, come in to my side, whereupon I shall have my hands ready to receive and sit him in the normal way. So watch carefully.

'Buffy, heel! I turn him in. Good dog! Now slightly away as I bend and stretch. Now in towards me. I take my left foot forward and, with my hands ready, I say "Sit! Good dog!". And as you can see, I got the dog to come from that crooked position into this straight one beside me. I did it by using my voice, with left hand on the leash and accurate footwork.' **(Fig. 19)**

The instructor can demonstrate this two or three times, always facing the same way as the handlers so that they can follow the footwork in particular. If the instructor faced the handlers, they would find the footwork harder to follow.

You will find the same instructional technique used in schools of dancing. The instructor stands out in front of the pupils and facing the same way, and explains and demonstrates the dance. The pupils follow the steps, the timing, and so on.

It is quite a good idea to split the class by having one team behind the other, so that the rear team can watch. An easy way to get all the dogs in the front team to sit crooked in relation to the handlers is to ask the handlers to turn to face to the right so that they are one behind the other with their dogs sitting beside them. Then if the handlers tell their dogs to stay while they turn to face the left, all the handlers will be abreast of each other and all their dogs will be crooked. This makes it look realistic. The instructor can then give individual tuition to every handler in turn, starting with the person at the right-hand end. When they have all done it, they can swap places with the other team and watch them do it.

wide sits

A dog that sits wide usually heels wide, and if the sit is wide, the stand and drop

Dog sitting in a crooked position.

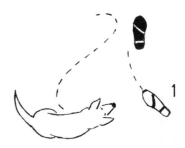

The handler's right foot remains still while the left foot is taken back in an arc; simultaneously the dog is led with the left hand as indicated.

As the dog turns towards the handler's left foot, that foot is taken forward to the right foot. The dog follows and is made to sit straight and close beside the handler.

Fig. 19.   Correcting the crooked sit

will be affected in the same way. If a dog has this fault, the first thing to do is to impress it upon the handler to walk straight and not into the dog. The second thing is to explain and demonstrate how a wide-sit correction works.

Dog sitting straight but wide of the handler.

The handler's left foot is taken back in an arc and, as the dog is turned in towards it, the right foot takes a pace sideways to the right.

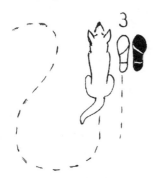

The left foot is taken forwards to the right foot. The dog follows and is made to sit close to the handler's side.

Fig. 20. Correcting the wide sit

The correction is the same as for the crooked sit, up to the point where you turn the dog in towards you (just when you are about to take your left foot forward); but before you move your left foot, take a pace sideways to the right with your right foot, then take your left foot forward and against the right foot (**Fig. 20**).

You will notice that both you and your dog have shifted over sideways to the right of your original positions. You have in fact drawn your dog closer to you. When you do this correction you can say 'Heel close!' and the extra word 'close' will prove to be of great value in the future.

If a dog has a habit of walking wide this method can be applied when going forward, while heeling, and when coming to a halt in the sit, stand or drop position. You need to have an open piece of ground for this, as you will be walking in progressive parallel lines to your right (**Fig. 21**).

After some time your dog will not go through the whole procedure you have taught it in the crooked-sit or wide-sit correction. Instead, it will do a shortcut by shuffling in to your side and sitting straight—which after all is exactly what you want.

The pattern you and your dog have learnt in carrying out the crooked-sit correction can also be used when you want to recall your dog to heel. Imagine you are free-walking your dog. It is on the full length of the leash and you stop. You want to bring your dog to heel, but it is too far away for you to take hold of the clip part of the leash. So form a sort of ring, with your left thumb and first finger loosely around the leash. Put your hands down to the dog's height, command enthusiastically 'Heel!' and as soon as your dog responds say 'Good dog' and pull the leash through with your right hand, which is holding the handle of the leash. As the leash comes through your left thumb and first finger, grip it near the clip and carry out the procedure of the crooked-sit correction.

In weeks to come you will be able to do this off the leash; but continue to use your voice with left hand and foot actions.

(iii)

The same procedure can be applied when coming to a halt.

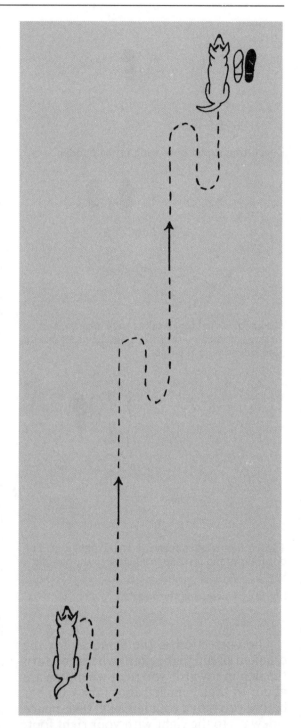

(ii)

As they walk together the handler can include the same procedure and continue forward.

(i)

With the dog sitting beside the handler, the command 'Heel' is given and the handler carries out the procedure shown in Fig. 20, but this time continues to walk forwards.

Fig. 21.   Correcting a dog that heels wide

Later you can bring your dog to heel from a greater distance, and finally call it to heel while you are walking; but in both cases continue to use your left hand in company with your voice.

the finish to the recall

Many years ago the common method of bringing a dog around to heel after it had come and sat in front of you was to say 'Heel!' and give it a series of little jerks on the leash. This gradually brought the dog around the back of its handler until it was told to sit as it reached the handler's left side. The dog did this finish satisfactorily, but with some reluctance because it received repeated jerks on the leash.

Then another method was introduced, whereby the handler took a step back with the right foot as the word 'Heel!' was given. This enticed the dog to move around the handler, and as it got halfway the handler brought the right foot forward again, causing the dog to turn and come forward to sit at the handler's left side. This method certainly did away with lots of little jerks, but dogs developed a habit of going very wide around the backs of the handlers, even when they did not step back.

So in the early 1960s I devised and tried out a new method to eliminate the fault of dogs going wide. Instead of stepping back, I told the dog to stay while I stepped

Fig. 22.   Finish to the recall. Imagine the dog has just been recalled, sat in front and praised. Tell it to stay, step forward on its right side close to its tail so that your feet are facing the spot in the distance from where it has come. Pass the leash from right to left hand behind you. Put your head down and around to your left and invite the dog to heel. Sit it and praise.

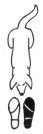

Dog sitting in front of the handler.

The handler takes a short pace forward with the right foot, straight and close to the dog.

As the left foot is taken close to the right foot, the handler commands the dog to 'Heel' and then to 'Sit' straight and close.

Later the handler stands quite still, commands and signals with the right hand for the dog to heel. The dog will then respond to these alone.

Fig. 23.   Subsequent steps to the finish

forward with my right foot first, then with my left foot, to stand on the dog's right side, straight, close and just past its hindquarters. I passed the leash from right hand to left behind my back and, leaning forward and turning my head to the *left* and downward under my left arm, said 'Heel!'. The dog naturally thought I was going for a walk in that direction. Not wishing to be left behind, it instantly followed the direction from which my voice came and joined me at my left side by the shortest route **(Fig. 22)**. When I felt that the dog understood this exercise, I took only half a pace forward with both feet, and later only a quarter of a pace; finally I made no movement, and the dog responded perfectly to just the command 'Heel!' and a little hand-signal with my right hand close round my right leg. So with careful foot positioning you can get your dog to finish closely and willingly without a jerk, but always be ready to mould your dog into a perfect sit at your side **(Fig. 23)**.

When showing handlers in a class how to do this finish, not much explanation is required and it is not really necessary to give a demonstration. The whole thing can be done in the practical work. All that the instructor needs to say is:

'I am now going to show you how to bring your dogs around to heel after they have completed a recall. Since you are all in a line abreast of each other with your dogs sitting at heel, tell them to stay and then turn around to face them. That's good! Stand quite close to them. Now imagine you have just recalled your dog and praised it for sitting in front of you. Tell your dog to stay and step forward on its right side close to its tail so that your feet are facing the spot in the distance from where the dog has come. Pass your leash from your right hand to your left behind your back. Put your head down and around to your *left* side and invite your dog to heel, and as it comes around the back of you, praise the dog, sit it, and praise again.'

The instructor should advise handlers to treat this as a separate exercise for the time being and not to attach it too often to the end of the recall. Otherwise dogs are inclined to do the recall and the finish all in one without sitting in front of the handler. As time goes on the finishes can be attached more frequently.

continental finish

In the early 1950s I saw another kind of finish being used in British competitions, but only by a few people. Today it is quite fashionable in Great Britain, the USA and many other countries. As far as I know it started in Europe and is, in my opinion, a very smart finish indeed. Somehow it has earned the name 'continental finish' in Great Britain, and I shall refer to it that way as well. Anyone who has learnt the routine foot and hand movement in correcting a crooked sit will find this finish very easy:

'Handlers, last week I showed you how to do the finish to the recall, by getting the dogs to heel around the back of you and to sit beside you. Today I'll show you how to bring them to your side the other way, which is known as a continental finish. If you would like to try this, just follow my instructions. Tell your dog to stay and turn around to face it. That's good! Imagine that it has just done the recall. Hold the clip part of the leash in your left hand, invite the dog to heel, cast your left foot back in an arc, and bring your dog to heel just as you do in carrying out a correction for a crooked sit. And that's all there is to it. **(Fig. 24)**

'As time goes on and your dog really understands what you want it to do, you won't have to put your foot back so far, and finally not at all. Now you may think that by teaching both fin-

Dog sitting in front of the handler.

The handler's right foot remains still while the left foot is taken back in an arc; simultaneously the dog is led with the left hand as indicated.

As the dog turns towards the handler's left foot, that foot is taken forward to the right foot. The dog follows and is made to sit straight beside the handler.

Fig. 24.   Continental finish

ishes you will confuse your dog as to which one you want. Well, I can assure you that you won't. The command "Heel!" is the same in both, but the thing that determines which way you want your dog to heel is your hand-signal. If you use your right hand, the dog will go around the back of you; if you use your left hand, the dog will go to your left side by swinging its hindquarters around in a semicircle.'

In Australian obedience trials all dogs are required to finish by going around the back of the handler. However, there is nothing to stop you doing both finishes in general work. One very good effect of this is that the dog is kept guessing which finish the handler will want. Consequently it plays safe and comes in straight.

As I mentioned earlier, some dogs are inclined to do the recall and finish all in one without sitting in front of the handler, or if they do sit it is slightly over to the handler's right.

left-about turn

There are two recognised ways of doing this turn. One way is known as the pivot turn, in which you do a left-about turn but the dog does a right-about turn. All you have to do is transfer the leash from one hand to the other and back as you turn. Although most people prefer this turn because it is easy, I prefer the other, where both handler and dog do a left-about turn. My reason is that you have not taught the dog anything new the first way, because it has already learnt how to do a right-about turn. I always like to teach my dogs as many different manoeuvres as I can.

I believe instructors should explain and demonstrate both ways of doing the left-about turn, and that it should then be left to each handler to choose which method to learn and use. Actually, I don't bother to show handlers either of these left-about turns if they just want basic training. I show them only to those who want to go in for obedience trials.

As the left hand takes hold of the clip part of the leash, the handler spins around on the left toe to face the dog.

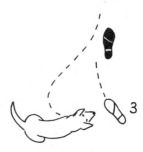

The handler moves the left foot back in an arc and guides the dog as indicated.

The handler steps forward with the left foot and continues to walk as the dog keeps to heel.

Fig. 25.   Left-about turn

As I said earlier, the pivot turn is easy but the other one needs a little bit of explanation with a demonstration across in front of the class backwards and forwards a few times:

'Today I am going to show you the other way of doing the left-about turn. You will notice that the continental finish is incorporated in this turn. As I walk across in front of you all, I prepare for this left-about turn by taking hold of the clip part of the leash with my left hand. I give the command "Heel" in a melodious tone, and spin on my left toe 180° to face the dog, bringing my right foot around too.'

It is best for the instructor to stand still a moment before doing the second part:

'I now cast my left foot back, bringing the dog around as if doing a continental finish, but as I bring my left foot forward I let go of the clip part of the leash, praise, and keep walking.' (Fig. 25)

The instructor should demonstrate this twice, breaking up each turn into two parts, before doing two more without the pause in the middle of each. Then the handlers can see the way it all flows together.

It does not take long for your dog to learn that it has to revolve with you as you left-about turn, and it will soon know which turn you are going to make by the intonation of your command. Later your dog will recognise a left-about turn by the way you turn your entire body 180° to the left. Eventually, you will not even have to give the clue in the tone of your voice, or use your left hand and foot as a guide. The dog will just revolve with you as it sees you turn in that direction. This turn is very easy to do when you know how, but you should not attempt to do it until you have mastered all the other basic moves in heelwork.

So you can see how good footwork is so important in heelwork. The correction of the crooked sit is the first one to learn and all the others follow on from it.

11

retrieving

Running after something and picking it up can be great fun for a dog. The only trouble is that the dog will not always want to come back to you with the object, let alone give it up. Retrieving is the big stepping-stone to advanced work: once taught, it opens up a wide new world of exercises you and your dog can enjoy.

Where do you start? When? How? With what?

I have always believed that the first stages of retrieving should be taught as early as possible. You can even start with a puppy of ten to eleven weeks. Take a small piece of rolled-up soft leather with an elastic band around it and, crouching down on the floor in a small room with doors closed, rub your hands around it to transmit your natural body scent to it as you mysteriously talk to the puppy to arouse its interest. Then gently throw the bundle along the ground to about half a metre (18 in.) away and tell it 'Fetch!'. Nearly every lively puppy, being so curious, will run after it and pick it up; as he does so, praise the puppy 'Very good boy!'. He may bring it back, or he may run around with it —it doesn't really matter. The important thing is that he has run after it and picked it up, you have praised him and he likes it. You have made a start. Do it only twice,

then put the article mysteriously and slowly away in your pocket. Let him see it disappear: he will probably still want it. Do exactly the same thing the next day. It will then become his special treat.

To teach dogs to retrieve in a dog-club situation is not always easy, for the simple reason that there are so many distractions around. Nevertheless instructors should show handlers how to do it, even if they don't get any results at the time. Handlers can then practise the retrieve at home during the week.

Actually, I believe retrieving should be taught in Class II—to those who want to learn it. It may well be that there are only a few who want to teach their dogs to retrieve—in which case arrangements could be made for another instructor, preferably an experienced one, to take those few handlers and dogs aside and show them what to do. As soon as they have finished they could return to their class.

The reason why I suggest that retrieving should start in Class II is that in Class I dogs should have learnt the very basics: heelwork (which includes forward, sit and the three turns), the sit-stay and the recall. Handlers should by now have fairly good control of their dogs. Also, the dogs will not have had too much heelwork pumped into them, which can lower a dog's degree of initiative. That initiative is essential for learning the retrieve.

In any class where dogs are learning the retrieve, at whatever stage, the instructor should make it the first exercise of the day —when the dog is wide awake and most alert. If it is given other exercises beforehand, like a lot of monotonous heelwork, the dog may be somewhat mentally drained and may not have the interest to retrieve. When dogs have been taught to retrieve and they reach higher classes, the exercise can be inserted more or less anywhere during the training session. That is all right with those dogs because they know exactly what to do; but we have to play safe with young dogs who are in the early stages of learning the exercise, and that is why instructors should make it the first exercise of the day.

It doesn't matter what you use as a retrieve article. It could be a rolled-up piece of leather, a glove, a short piece of rod, a pair of socks together turned inside out—anything will do as long as it is something that you think your dog likes holding.

The retrieve is a very easy exercise for the instructor to explain, but it is not so easy to demonstrate with a borrowed dog, unless of course the dog has got to know the instructor fairly well. A borrowed Labrador, however, is a pretty safe bet, because it is a gun-dog breed with a natural instinct to retrieve, and is so immediately adaptable that it will work for virtually anyone.

The instructor should explain the retrieve exercise to the class along these lines:

'The first exercise I shall show you today will be the first stage of the retrieve. Fiona has kindly lent me her Labrador, Ben, with whom I'll demonstrate. With Ben relaxed on my left side but not strictly at heel, I hold the handle of the leash plus one more point down the leash in my left hand, with no more than half a metre of leash between us. I take hold of the *very end* of this piece of rolled-up leather in my right hand. I shall now tease the dog up using an excitable voice and move around two or three times on this spot, keeping the article up high. Hopefully, his interest will be aroused, he will leap up to grab the article, and when he does I shall let him have it and praise him and trot around in a huge circle with a radius of 10 metres. I shall continue to praise him ensuring the leash is kept just slack. While trotting and just before I return to you, I shall shorten the leash down to the clip, which will make it easier for me to reach down with my right hand, take hold of the end of the article, stop, and say "Give!". As soon as Ben opens his mouth I'll praise him. Then I will do it once more as before. When I have taken the object off him the second time, I shall hide it away slowly and mysteriously in one of my pockets. He will probably want it again and leap up to get it. If he does, that is a very good note on which to finish: it will keep him hungry for it, so that next time I produce it he will be rearing to get it again.

'If by any chance Ben does not respond, I will ask Fiona to try it, because a dog is more likely to do it for its owner than for someone it does not know so well. My main job here is to show you what to do; the rest is up to you. I am of course quite willing to try it with another of the dogs you have kindly offered to me.'

When it comes to the practical I always make a point of telling handlers not to worry if their dogs do not respond. The important thing is that they, the handlers, know what to do. After answering any questions, the advice I would give to all the handlers for the week would be as follows:

'Don't overdo it. Two retrieves with a large run-around each day are enough at this stage. Always run clockwise and not anticlockwise or you will be running into the dog. If the dog ever drops the object, never, *never* tell him off; just pick it up and get him to do it again. If you tell the dog off in any way, it is likely to put him off retrieving anything. Also, try to pick a time of day when you think he is most excited. This may be first thing in the morning, or the moment the dog sees you arrive home from work. I chose the after-work time with one of my Border Collies some years ago. I could do it only twice before her excitability subsided, and it took some months before she could do the full exercise. When she got the idea, though, she loved doing it again and again. So you see, you do have to be very patient.'

Provided the dogs are showing satisfactory results by the following lesson, the instructor should then show the class the next stage. After teasing the dog up as before to get it really keen, the handler should throw the article no more than 3 metres straight out in front, saying 'Fetch!' and going with the dog, allowing it to run after the article to pick it up. As the dog goes after it, the handler should release the second part of the leash from the left hand. As soon as the article is picked up, the handler should praise with 'Good dog!' followed immediately by 'Come! Good dog!' and should walk backwards along the exact line on which they went forward. The article should be taken from the dog while the handler is walking backwards. There is no need to sit the dog. If that is attempted at this stage, the dog is likely to drop the article, and that would be a great pity. The handler needs to achieve taking it, before the dog achieves dropping it. At this stage it is vitally important to get the main task established in the dog's mind, and for that task to be accomplished with great eagerness and joy.

In all the obedience tests and working trials in England, all dogs have to retrieve.

Because of this the retrieve is taught as early as possible so that people can enter the competitions. In the USA and Australia the rules are different. In the novice trials dogs are not required to retrieve, but in the higher trials they are. I have found that many handlers in Australia have struggled through the novice trials to gain the required three passes, which qualify them for a Companion Dog title, before they have thought about teaching their dogs to retrieve so that they can train for and enter the open trials. When the retrieve training is put off until this time it often proves too late. My advice to handlers interested in competitive work is to start teaching their dogs to retrieve at an early stage, even before they enter a novice trial.

A few years ago I held a special weekend course for novice handlers in one of Victoria's dog-training clubs. On the Friday evening I gave them a lecture on all the exercises, and on the Saturday morning I showed them, and got them to do, the first stage of the retrieve. Most of the dogs were young and had been attending for no more than six weeks or so. The first stage went extremely well and the dogs really loved doing it; needless to say every handler was elated. So on the Sunday morning I decided to do the second stage and let each do it twice. Then I decided to try one more thing. I set up the high jump with just the baseboard, and gave the class a demonstration with an imaginary dog. I threw the article out and walked backwards as described and everyone understood what they had to do. Then I asked them to do the second retrieve immediately while conveniently near the high jump, so that they could whirl around just once about half a metre (18 in.) from the baseboard to get the dog keen, and toss their article just over the jump to land no more than half a metre from it on the other side. I was confident that each dog would jump over the baseboard, pick up the article and come back over the baseboard to its handler on the command 'Come!'. Well, I am pleased to say that every dog did it, including one dog that had been attending the club for about eighteen months, whose handler had had no success in teaching it to retrieve.

I showed this method at two seminars in the United States, and at the second one, in Houston, Texas, I struck a slight problem. I asked if someone would like to lend me a dog, and accepted the first offer, a lovely Bulldog. Well, I tried to get it teased up and interested in the article I had, but it was not interested at all. After a few unsuccessful attempts I was on the point of thanking the owner for her kind offer and asking for another dog, when I decided on impulse to try something I had never tried before: I made a snorting sound, similar to the sound a Bulldog makes—and was surprised to see that it responded with some interest. So I did it again and again and started to jig around, and within seconds the dog had become quite excited, as if to say 'You can come to Texas any ol' time'. Then it got interested in the article and I tossed it a few steps away, whereupon the dog ran straight out, picked it up, came to me and let me take it. I continued talking to the dog, making lots of nice snorting sounds to which it continued to respond. Then I tossed the article just over the baseboard of the high jump. The Bulldog sprang straight over, scooped it up and returned to me over the jump—to a round of applause from the audience of some seventy people. I praised the dog and finished on that good note, thanking the owner for lending me her dog. I learnt later that this was the first time it had retrieved.

Well, handlers may in time imitate their instructors when using their voices, but I never thought I'd have to imitate a dog to get it interested in doing a retrieve!

12

puppy class

When I first came to Australia I couldn't find a dog-training club that had a class for puppies—though I should add that there weren't anywhere near as many clubs as there are today. In those days a dog had to be at least six months old before it could attend training, so you could say that adult pups were being trained. Did that meet the needs of all owners? No, not really, because by the time some pups reached five months they were out of hand and becoming liabilities.

I for one was advocating in lectures that there should be training classes for puppies and their owners, so that many of the problems that otherwise develop could be prevented. It has been very pleasing to see more and more clubs introduce puppy-training classes into their programmes, with excellent results.

The main purpose and greatest advantage of having a puppy class is to provide the opportunity for puppies to socialise, and to meet and be handled by other people.

The instructor's main task is to show handlers how to talk to their puppies, how to introduce them to other puppies, people and things, how to handle them on their leashes, how to encourage and praise them, and how to correct them when

necessary. Because they are so young, puppies cannot concentrate for too long and are very prone to distractions around them. Therefore it would be difficult to attempt something like heelwork, and it is better to move them around by just free-walking them.

The instructor should explain and demonstrate how the leash should be held up, not tight but just slack, so that if at any time the puppy wants to turn around, it can revolve underneath the leash without getting its legs tangled in it. Great care should also be taken to ensure that when two puppies meet their leashes do not twist and lock; if they do, one or both puppies will start to panic and they will probably snap at each other.

Even though strict heelwork is not given, it is surprising how many other little exercises can be taught. To begin, the instructor should explain the first principles of training: Command, Action, Response and Praise. It is essential that everyone learn this. Then the instructor can demonstrate how to sit the puppies, which can be very useful before crossing roads, for example, during daily walks.

Handlers can also be shown how to stand their puppies, an easy exercise. A very good and practical time for this is when they are grooming them on tables. It is a good idea for the instructor to demonstrate this on a table. Imagine that the puppy is sitting on the table. Hold it by the collar in the right hand and, with the left hand under its belly, say in a quiet melodious tone 'Stand!', and lift up gently. As it responds by stepping backwards with its hind feet, praise 'Good dog!' **(Fig. 26)**.

The drop can also be taught. This could be done on the grass, so that the puppy associates the exercise with having to lie down on the grass. A good time to do it is towards the end of the lesson when the puppy is somewhat tired and will therefore be quite ready for the exercise. It is a very simple exercise for a puppy. The instructor first places the borrowed puppy on his or her (i.e. the instructor's) left side:

'Handlers, to teach a puppy to lie down, all you have to do is place your left hand on its shoulders, with your thumb on its right shoulderblade and your fingers on its left shoulderblade. Then take hold of its right foreleg at the knee-joint with the thumb and first finger of your right hand. Lift it up a little and take it close to its left foreleg, and take hold of that one between your first and second fingers. Say "Drop!" and lift both front legs up underneath its lower jaw, at the same time pressing down very gently with your left hand, guiding the body down and into a straight position **(Fig. 27)**. The moment the puppy is down, let go of its paws, turn your right hand around the other way, and praise it with your voice and with slow gentle strokes from the point of its chin to its chest. Always praise under the chin like this, as this will act as an incentive for the puppy to go down and remain down. If you praise the puppy on top of its head it might like that as well and, perhaps wanting more, might get up, which is not the idea. Retain your left hand lightly on its shoulders in case it tries to arise. If it does, your hand is in perfect position to push down again **(Fig. 28)**. After about five seconds, dismiss the puppy with "Go free!" and let it relax.'

The instructor should suggest to the handlers that they do this drop exercise two or three times every evening and on carpet, where it is comfortable for the puppy to drop. It is important that the puppy associate the exercise with pleasure; it should not be used as an exercise of submission. It helps if the puppy, during its early days of training, is taught these three exercises in three different situ-

Fig. 26. To teach a puppy to stand without creeping forward, hold its front with the right hand, say in a quiet melodious tone 'Stand' and, with the left hand under its belly, lift up gently. As it responds by stepping backwards with its hind feet, praise with 'Good dog!'.

Fig. 27.   Teaching a puppy to drop. With the left hand on the puppy's shoulders, say 'Drop' and lift its front legs up underneath its lower jaw with the right hand.

Fig. 28.   Retain the left hand lightly on its shoulders in case it tries to arise. Praise it under the chin with the right hand.

ations: sit at the kerb, stand on the grooming table and drop on the carpet. Later it will do all three anywhere at any time.

The recall can also be taught in a puppy class, but in a different way from that explained in earlier chapters. The handler can leave the puppy with the instructor and walk away a few metres, and because the puppy is so dependent upon and attached to its handler, its natural reaction is to want to follow. It is best for the instructor to talk to and slowly stroke the puppy to reassure it while holding it on the leash as the handler walks away. As soon as the handler calls the puppy, the instructor should release it. Praising the puppy all the way, the handler can take hold of the

leash near the clip, at the same time walking backwards a few steps, and bring the puppy into the sit position in the normal way, as explained earlier in this book. This type of training, in which the puppy's natural affection for its handler is being used, will help tremendously when it comes to doing recalls from a sit-stay position and when free-walking in Class I.

A lot of time in a puppy class will be taken up with the asking of questions, and these of course are to be expected. The advice that an instructor can give can prevent many faults developing and save a lot of work later. Two common problems that handlers have with their puppies are mouthing and jumping up at them or at other people. The instructor should answer very simply by advising handlers to correct a puppy for these misdemeanours, and others like them, by taking hold of it with both hands each side of the neck, saying 'No!' and giving a quick shake— which is how a bitch will correct her puppies! They do not become afraid of her or challenge her; they respect her for it. If handlers do the same, the same results will be achieved.

Chewing things is another problem. This can be corrected in the same way, if the puppy can be caught in the act of chewing. Instructors should also advise handlers to remove all accessible chewable items that puppies might take a fancy to, and to make sure that they have plenty of their own toys to play with.

Some handlers may be keen to get their dogs to retrieve. If this is the case, the instructor can give advice on how handlers can start in the seclusion of their own homes, as covered in the early part of the chapter on retrieving.

Instructing a puppy class is quite different from instructing in the other obedience classes. You need to keep it particularly relaxed and enjoyable, for handlers as well as puppies. It is a fascinating class, and you can learn so much just by watching the numerous reactions of puppies and how they gain confidence week after week. It is a class that calls for a lot of flexibility, and one that should provide lots and lots of fun to handlers, puppies and instructor alike.

13

stand and stand for examination

When explaining the stand exercise, the instructor can begin by saying something like this:

'The stand exercise is one of the easiest obedience exercises to teach a dog. You may wonder why we don't teach it before we teach the sit. There are two reasons: firstly, the sit is considered far more important, as you will have realised from previous lessons, and it is also the most frequently used exercise in obedience trials. Secondly, the dog is more likely to move in the stand position when told to stay, whereas it is more stable in the sit position.

'I shall now demonstrate how to do the stand with Jenny's dog Bree, whom she has kindly lent me for this purpose. I'll demonstrate this a few times as I walk from your right across in front of the class. So would you please imagine that I am actually walking along with the dog at heel. I decide to stand the dog. I have its attention. I now prepare by putting the clip part of the leash into my right hand; I hold my left arm over the dog's body and I say "Stand!", which is followed immediately by an action with both hands simultaneously: my right hand gives a quick horizontal jerk back on the leash (like you use in the left turn) and I lock the dog's left hind leg back with my left hand. Can you all see how the front of the left hind leg, which is called the stifle, fits neatly into my cupped hand? You will also notice that the lower part of my forearm is against the left side of the dog's body. This helps to keep the dog facing straight between my left arm and left leg. As soon as the dog responds, I praise her "Good girl!"; at the same time I let go of the clip part of the leash, take my left hand off her stifle and stroke her head gently. Now I shall do this a few times as I walk across in front of you, so please watch very carefully.'

After the instructor has completed the demonstration, he or she can get the handlers, one by one, to do two stands each, before doing the exercise together as a class.

Handlers in most obedience clubs are taught to say 'Stand!' and, holding the dog back a bit on the leash in the left hand, to bring the right hand around to the dog's nose as a signal. The result is that, in most cases, the dog stops but creeps forward an extra pace to the handler's signalling hand. I do not use a hand-signal when teaching a dog to stand—I would if I had three hands, but I haven't! So I always make full use of the two I have and apply them physically on the dog to get an instant response and teach it to stand accurately, just as I would with the sit.

When the dog has learnt to stand on my command, without my having to use my hands, I then accompany the command with a hand-signal. Later, in more advanced training, I gradually reduce my vocal command to a mere 'St . . .!' with a hand-signal; and finally I use the hand-signal without any sound whatever. And as soon as the dog stands on signal alone, I always give praise. It's as easy as that—provided the dog is shown right from the start precisely what it has to do.

Once a dog has been taught to stand, the exercise can be taken one stage further by being made into a stand-stay: you leave the dog and come out in front to stand facing it. This is usually very easy because you have already taught the dog to do a sit-stay. By combining two exercises it has learnt at different times—to stand in heelwork and to understand the stay—you now have the stand-stay, which will be used later in the stand-stay for examination.

You will notice that I said 'later'. I wish to stress this point and explain why. If an instructor told handlers to stand their dogs and leave them by coming out in front of them, and then approached each dog in turn to examine it, a number of dogs, particularly the timid ones, would be likely to move away because they felt threatened by the approach of the instructor. I have found this to be one of the biggest mistakes instructors make—and only because they don't realise how some dogs see them and how they will react in certain situations. It's all right for judges to walk up and examine dogs that are working and competing in the ring—because they have been trained and are sound in temperament, or at least should be. But when you are training you are training; you are not in a trial.

So how can we prevent things going wrong—the instructors making mistakes, the handlers becoming downhearted because their dogs move, and the dogs becoming worried about the exercise week after week? Well, it's not really very difficult. There are six stages towards the stand for examination through which the instructor can take the handlers and dogs.

Stage 1. The instructor should ask each handler in turn to stroll up (with the dog on a loose lead, not at heel but walking freely), to talk to the dog and allow it to sniff the instructor, and to move around. As the dog does this, the instructor should also talk to the dog, stroke it gently and observe its temperament. If this is all right, they can progress to Stage 2 the following week.

Stage 2. The handler should be asked to heel the dog forward and stand it just next to the instructor, who, without moving, should allow the dog to sniff the hand, and should then give the dog a few slow, gentle strokes under its chin, down the left side of its neck and perhaps along the top of its shoulders to halfway down its back. It is also a good idea for the instructor to allow the dog to rest its chin in the left hand while stroking the dog with the right. This simple handling technique helps a dog to feel more at ease while being examined. The handler, still beside the dog, also gives it confidence. Should the dog move for any reason, the handler is in the ideal position to carry out the necessary correction and make the dog stand again.

Stage 3. The handler should be asked to heel the dog and stand it next to the instructor, who has remained quite still. The examination can then be carried out as in Stage 2, but after about ten seconds the instructor can ask the handler to leave the dog with the command 'Stay!' and stand in front facing it, no more than half a metre (18 in.) away. After about ten seconds the handler should return, praise the dog and dismiss it.

Stage 4. With the progress being made, the instructor can ask the handler to heel the dog forward and stand it about 1½ metres (4½ ft) away. The instructor can then make that short approach to the dog from a slight angle, not from directly in front. The rest of the exercise can be carried out as in Stage 3.

Stage 5. With more progress now being made, the handler can stand the dog nearly 3 metres away from the instructor, tell the dog 'Stay!', and stand a little further out in front of it. The instructor can approach and carry out the examination as before, and also walk around the back of the dog and examine it from the other side. Then the handler can return to the dog by walking around the back of it.

Stage 6. When the instructor and the handler are quite confident that the dog will stand, stay and not mind being examined, it can be done off the leash. And as time goes on, the distances and durations can be gradually extended.

Well, you see how easy it is if you go about it gradually. Naturally all dogs are different, so you can't expect them all to advance at the same rate. It is therefore the responsibility of the instructor to work at the stage a dog is up to or ready for. Some dogs go through fairly quickly, others take a little time.

I think it would be appropriate for me to mention here a point about testing dogs when they are promoted from one class to the next in an obedience club.

Many clubs have a system of periodically holding testing days. Handlers and dogs in every class (except the top class)

have a number of exercises to do. If all are satisfactorily completed, the dog is promoted to the next class at the next training session. But if the dog passes, say, five of the six exercises, it stays in that class for several weeks, sometimes until the next testing day. Quite often the exercise the dog fails is the stand for examination. This happened to me once. Because my Border Collie was so friendly with the instructors, in fact with everyone, she moved to make a fuss of the examiner during the test. It didn't bother me: she was after all only seven months old at the time and I knew it wouldn't be long before she settled down. And in any case, I would much rather have a dog move out of friendliness than through being nervous or (worse still) aggressive. However, I was promptly informed that the dog had failed and would have to take the test again in so many weeks' time.

While tests like these are all right in theory, I don't believe they are so good in practice. A dog can always have an off day, just as we can, and I know that some handlers get very tense when under the pressure of a test and their tenseness can so easily be transmitted to their dogs.

I honestly believe the best way to promote dogs and handlers is to watch their general performance, taken as an *overall* performance. I believe in judging a handler and a dog on their merits. So if the dog was quite satisfactory on five out of six exercises, I would look at the exercise on which the dog failed, see what progress had been made and gauge how the handler was coping with it. The fact that the handler had trained the dog to do the other exercises satisfactorily would indicate that, given time, success would be achieved, so I would promote handler and dog to the next class.

People sometimes ask what is the purpose or advantage of teaching a dog to stand. I have heard that answered bluntly, 'It's in the obedience trials so you've got to do it!' Well, sure it's in the trials, but I always like to look at these exercises from a practical point of view.

Supposing you were heeling your dog and had to stop in very bad, wet, muddy, slippery conditions. Would you make your dog sit? Wouldn't it be nicer to stand your dog? And supposing you had to stop at a kerb with scores of pedestrians around you in a busy city. If the dog sat, someone might tread on its tail; so you would stand the dog instead. And when standing there waiting for the lights to change, what if some children stopped to admire your dog or started stroking it? Well, if you had taught it to stand for examination you'd have little cause for concern.

A few years ago I took my German Shepherd for a long walk in one of our huge parks. During the walk I wanted to pay a visit to the toilet, so I called Jade to heel and dropped her about 25 metres from the toilet block, told her to stay and went inside. When I came out a few minutes later I peered slowly around the corner of the building to see if she was still in the down position. Sure enough she was. She couldn't see me, but I could see the rear half of her body. So I decided to stay there for another ten minutes. After a few minutes I peeped around the corner again, and she was still in the same position, but I saw a little hand going slowly down her back: a boy of about twelve was stroking her. Well, I thought, this is a good test! After a while I returned to my dog and said quite casually, 'Good evening, young fellow. I gather you like dogs.' 'Yes, I do,' he replied. 'Well, I don't mind you stroking my dog, even though she has been told to stay here until I return and tell her she can go off and play again. But may I give you a friendly word of advice? This dog won't bite you, but one day you might go up to a dog to stroke it and it might not like it. Always be very careful when approaching a dog you don't know.' He was a nice lad and thanked me, and as he rode away on his bicycle, I really was so glad I had taught my dog the stand for examination. In fact, on this occasion Jade had been given an examination in the down position—*and* while I was out of sight as well!

14

drop and drop on recall

I mentioned in Chapter 12 that you can teach puppies to drop when they are quite young, but only for a few seconds before dismissing them to go off and play again. You will find this quite easy as they are not strong enough at this age to resist and rebel against you. Also, when they are so young they are smaller and it is much easier to take hold of their little paws and lift them up gently, and push down gently on their shoulders.

However, when pups become adult pups and older they change and really start to have minds of their own. This can make it very difficult for the handlers, and most frustrating if they cannot get them to drop. Some adult dogs can become very concerned if their handlers try to make them drop too early in training. This can cause them to panic and snap at their handlers. Therefore it is far better to get the more important exercises done first: the basic heelwork, the sit-stay and the recall. By doing these first you should get respect from your dog, and it will gain much confidence in you. Then when it comes to teaching it to drop, you shouldn't have much trouble.

Why do we need to teach a dog to drop? Well, if you wanted your dog to stay for any length of time, it would be most unkind to leave it in the sit position. If you put it into the drop—or the down position, as it is also called—it can relax and even have a little snooze. The longest sit-stay in any trial is three minutes; stays beyond that time are always in the drop position.

Although there are a few different methods you can use when teaching a dog to drop, the one I favour is the same as that mentioned in Chapter 12; but you need to change your position and right-hand technique when doing this with a bigger dog.

'Have your dog sitting beside you. Have the clip part of the leash in your left hand and also place your left hand on the dog's shoulders. Turn to face the side of your dog. Bend down on your right knee. This will enable you to pass your right forearm behind your dog's right knee-joint and take hold of its left knee-joint with your thumb on the front. Say "Drop!" or "Down!" and lift its front legs up as you push down on its shoulder-blades with your left hand. Praise the dog immediately it drops, and stroke gently and slowly under its chin.' **(Fig. 29)**

That is all the instructor needs to say in explaining the exercise. If a demonstration is necessary, the instructor should accept a dog who knows that person fairly well and has a sound temperament. It is

Fig. 29. The drop. With the left hand on the dog's shoulders, pass the right arm behind its right foreleg and take hold of its left foreleg. Command 'Drop' and lift its legs up while pushing gently down on its shoulders.

finger into the ground directly under its chin, simultaneously pushing and guiding the dog down with your left hand on its shoulders, and praising in the normal way.

The next stage is to drop the dog while walking at heel (Fig. 30). If the instructor needs to demonstrate this, it is best done two or three times across in front of the class, the way the sit and stand were demonstrated. Once handlers have had several weeks' experience, it is not always necessary for the instructor to do it with a dog; an imaginary dog will do. This applies with many exercises from about this stage on, though sometimes a full demonstration will still be necessary—particularly if a handler is having difficulties, or requests further help.

Once the dog will drop down on command alone, the exercise can be done during free-running. It doesn't matter in which direction the dog is running. Give it the command to drop when it is about 3 metres away from you and go immediately to it to uphold your command if necessary, and to praise it. Then dismiss it and let it run around again. As progress is made you can drop the dog when it is further away, about an extra metre at a time. But each time you do, get up to it as quickly as you can and praise it. Then it will always associate the exercise with pleasure, because it will have been praised on the very spot where you commanded it to drop down. This can be a very useful exercise, as you never know when you might need it.

I would like to give advice to instructors and handlers here in connection with training for the drop on the recall in an open obedience trial. Play safe and don't introduce the exercise until the dog has gained its Companion Dog title, but by all

then best to demonstrate the exercise twice in front of the class, which can come together as a group rather than watching in a long line. The first demonstration can be given by having the dog face the group, so that they can see from the front how the dog's legs should be lifted. The second demonstration can be given with the dog facing across to the group's left, so that they can see from the side how the dog goes down. It is important that the instructor speak to the class and not into the ground when bending down to explain what to do.

It will take a few days before your dog gets the basic idea of dropping, just as it did with the sit and stand exercises. You should then be able to do it by saying 'Drop!' and pointing your right index

Fig. 30. Dropping a dog in heelwork. Command 'Drop' and signal straight down with the right hand. To uphold the command and signal, jerk the dog down with the right hand and/or push down at the shoulders with the left hand.

means teach the dog to drop while free-running. There is no harm in that; in fact it is very good. My reason for saying this is that when dogs are taught to drop on the recall, many of them start to anticipate the drop and slow down. This is a pity when a dog has been trained to do such a speedy recall. So get the first title and then put in the drop on the recall, but do it only very occasionally (perhaps once in every ten or twelve recalls) when you are training for open trial work.

To do this exercise carry out a simple recall, and when the dog gets about half-way command it to drop and simul-taneously use a hand-signal and run to-wards it. Running towards the dog has a good effect on it: it will know you are coming forward to uphold your command and of course to praise it, and it is less likely to creep further on, as some dogs do if given half a chance! However, a further word of advice here with highly sensitive dogs. Don't run all the way or you might disturb the dog and cause it to move away. Per-haps run for the first 2 metres and, as soon as you see the dog drop, walk slowly the rest of the way. Praise the dog gently. Tell it to stay. Walk backwards to your original calling position. Wait a second or two,

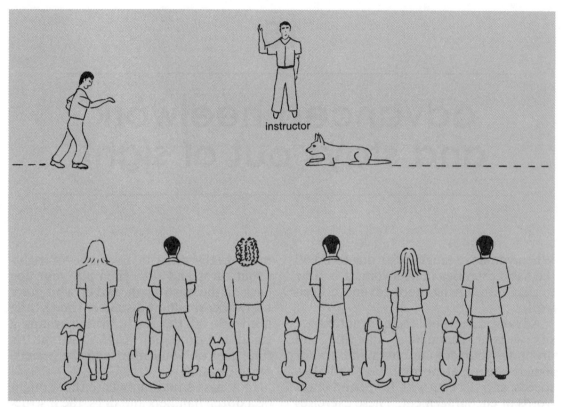

Fig. 31. The drop on recall. On the command and hand-signal to drop the dog, the handler proceeds to the dog to ensure that it drops and to praise it at the designated spot. Note the position of the instructor, who can watch the dog, instruct the handler and describe everything to the class.

then call your dog and praise it and finish in the normal way.

When you feel that the dog has mastered the exercise, there will be no need for you to go forward every time and praise it. By this time your dog will be quite happy about dropping, because you have praised it and made that an enjoyable part of the exercise.

The instructor needs to explain all these things when teaching this exercise in the advanced class. Once again, there is no need to use a dog for the demonstration; an imaginary dog can be used instead. But the instructor must *make* it real by using the right tone of voice, the hand-signal, the run and walk towards the dog, the vocal and physical praise, and so on. The exercise is best demonstrated, and the individual practical work best carried out, about 10 metres away across in front of the class, with the instructor on the far side facing the class (**Fig. 31**). All the handlers can then have a side view of every dog doing it, and the instructor is in the ideal position to watch the dog, instruct the handler and describe everything to the class. Although this exercise takes time, it is quite easy if taught progressively step by step.

15

advanced heelwork and stays out of sight

When you have taught your dog to do all the basic exercises in heelwork, it is time to start introducing more advanced heelwork.

Advanced heelwork includes automatic sits without commands; standing and dropping your dog on command and/or signal; heeling at normal, fast and slow speeds; and working with fewer and fewer words of encouragement. These exercises naturally demand more concentration from your dog as it watches your body and foot movements in all the turns you make, including the figure eight.

The first question many handlers ask is, 'When should I start heeling my dog off the leash?' The answer is, 'When you can heel it really well on the leash.' This means of course that it should respond to all the commands without having to be corrected on the leash.

The next question is, 'How should I start doing it?' Obviously, as with everything else in training, you should introduce it gradually.

If you are training on your own, heel your dog for a short distance, which might include a left and right turn and sit. Remove the leash discreetly. Do a little more heelwork with a couple of right-about turns and sits. Then put your dog back on the leash again, and do a bit more heelwork for a short distance. Then a little heelwork off the leash, with perhaps a stand and drop, and leave it at that. As time goes on you can extend the periods off the leash.

In a class situation, where there might be a dozen handlers and dogs, the instructor can ask every other handler to remove their leads and do a short stretch of heelwork, after which they can put their dogs back on their leashes while the others have a turn. By organising it this way only half the dogs in the class are working off the leash at any time, and the instructor is reducing the risk of anything going wrong. Imagine what might happen, with all the dogs working off the leash, if one of them bolted and incited the others to do the same!

When handlers enter this phase of working off the leash, the instructor should remind them of four main points:

1. Their number-one resource is their eyesight. They must watch their dogs all the time.

2. Their most important means of control is the voice.
3. Their hands should be used to uphold their commands when necessary.
4. They should always be ready to praise the dog the moment it has responded automatically without a command being given—for example, in the case of an automatic sit.

automatic sits

Many people say that they have great difficulty getting their dogs to sit without a command, or that it has taken them months to perfect it.

It is quite simple really, provided the dog will sit on command. Take it to an open space where you can sit it four times in a straight line. Sit the dog first, say 'Heel!', go forward 2 metres and sit it on command. Quickly praise. Say 'Heel!', go forward another 2 metres and sit the dog again. Repeat twice more, at 2-metre intervals, then come to an abrupt halt—and the dog should sit without a command. As soon as it sits automatically, praise it. So in that distance of 8 metres the dog has sat four times. The first, second and third sits were on the command 'Sit'. Because these were given rapidly within about ten seconds, it became a reflex action in the dog, so that when the fourth stop came it sat automatically. The whole thing was done within about twelve seconds. If the sits had been carried out with a distance of about 10 metres between them you would not have got the same result. The training has to be rapid, and over a short distance.

An instructor teaching a class this method of achieving an automatic sit should explain that when the order 'Halt!' is given there will be only a very short time —about one and a half seconds—before the order 'Forward!' is given. If handlers are forewarned about this, they will realise how fast they will have to be, and none of them will want to be the odd one who cannot do it! This instructional technique has two purposes: (1) to teach the automatic sits, and (2) to get the handlers to act quickly.

slow pace

This is very easy when your dog has been taught everything at normal speed. Avoid doing too much of it if the dog tends to lag or show a lack of willingness. In giving the command 'Heel' when you are about to step forward, lower your voice and draw out the word just a little. Not only will it keep a young dog calm, but it will in time warn your dog at which speed you are going to go forward.

fast pace

You should not attempt this until you know that you have absolute control over your dog at normal pace. When you are about to go forward at the fast pace, you can raise the pitch of your voice just slightly when you say 'Heel'. In time your dog will get to know at which speed you are going to go forward.

figure eight

I cannot see much practical value in this exercise. Many dogs find it very boring; they start to lose willingness and this results in lagging. I have seen some cunning dogs, who have worked many times in the obedience ring, stop between the two stewards, let the handlers go around one of them, and then rejoin the handlers on the way back! I also know of a few male dogs who have promptly lifted a leg on the steward or judge while coming around! I wouldn't bother to teach the exercise except to those who want to train for trials.

I always advise handlers who wish to do a figure eight to do it on an irregular pattern, not a set pattern where they are going around two people standing 3 metres apart. Imagine there are five or six people spaced out on an area equivalent to about half a tennis court. Heel your dog around them, encouraging it, especially when you curve around to the right, and keep up a good speed as you go around in an irregular pattern. Do it only about twice a week, not every day. Too much will just bore your dog.

zig-zag

A somewhat more practical exercise in heelwork—one that I first saw done in the obedience ring at Crufts Dog Show in England many years ago—is for competitors to heel their dogs off lead in a zig-zag through a line of special cones (witches' hats) and return through them, once up and once back. One could say it represents a handler and dog heeling among a lot of pedestrians in a shopping area.

Some dog-training clubs do the same sort of thing in heelwork, only they zig-zag through the class of handlers (**Fig. 32**). This routine is all right in an advanced class, where the dogs are reliable, but it is not one I would recommend for any of the lower classes. Instructors should take special note of this.

Firstly, it must be remembered that dogs in the lower classes have not had much training and their handlers are not very experienced. A number of the young dogs will be excitable, some may be timid and a few may have aggressive tendencies. If zig-zagging in heelwork is done among such dogs, there can be trouble. The close

work involved in weaving in and out gets the excitable dogs jumping around, the aggressive dogs stirred up and the timid ones very anxious. At the same time it makes a lot of handlers apprehensive.

If the routine is introduced into a class, it should be done with care. I always suggest that, as each dog passes between two others, there should be adequate space, and that the handler and dog should walk through at right-angles to the line of handlers, right turn, then right turn again, pass through the next two, left turn, then left turn again, pass through the next two, and so on. The handler heeling his or her dog should be watching and talking to it, either warning it if it is likely to be distracted, or encouraging it if it needs reassurance. The two handlers either side should be doing the same with their dogs, which are sitting beside them (**Fig. 33**).

intonation

I said much earlier that the word 'Heel', simply interpreted, means 'Accompany me at my side'. So it doesn't matter in which direction you go, or in what position the dog happens to be, when you call it to join you at your left side; you still use the same word. However, it is a command in dog training which can have a variety of intonations and these should be used according to the situation.

In basic heelwork two intonations are learnt by the novice handler in the first lesson. With 'Forward', 'Heel' needs to be said in an *inviting* tone; and it should be said in a *firm, corrective* tone if the dog needs to be corrected for pulling, as much as to say 'You get back to where you should be'. With the right-about and right turns, 'Heel' should be in a most *interesting* tone, as if to say 'I've got a special treat for you'. With the left turn, 'Heel' should

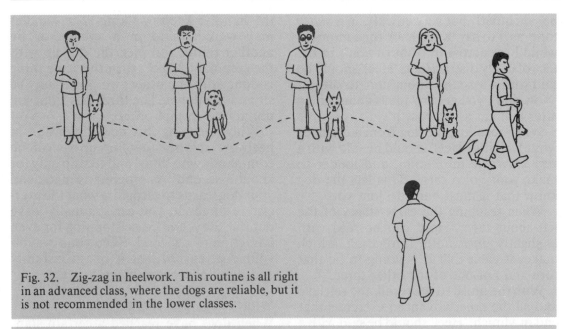

Fig. 32. Zig-zag in heelwork. This routine is all right in an advanced class, where the dogs are reliable, but it is not recommended in the lower classes.

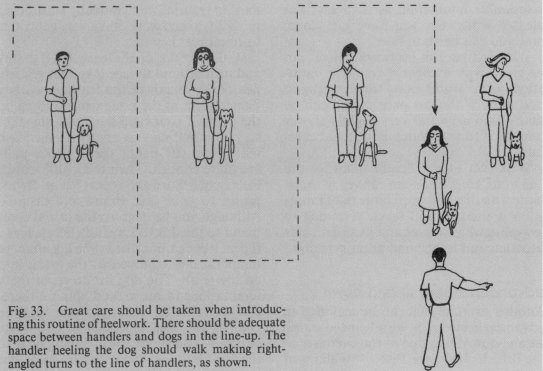

Fig. 33. Great care should be taken when introducing this routine of heelwork. There should be adequate space between handlers and dogs in the line-up. The handler heeling the dog should walk making right-angled turns to the line of handlers, as shown.

be said quietly but very quickly, in a *sharp* tone, as if to say 'Keep back for a moment while I get across in front of you'. In the face of likely distractions, 'Heel' should be said with a *warning* intonation, to suggest 'Now don't you get any ideas about going after that cat as we pass it'.

When recalling the dog from a distance while walking, 'Heel' should be said with a *very excitable* intonation, and louder to make your voice carry. This lets the dog know that it must hurry to join you.

When teaching the early stages of the left-about turn, 'Heel' can be said with a slightly *melodious* intonation which makes it clear that it is going to be that turn and not one of the other three.

With the finish to the recall, the retrieve and all the other advanced exercises that end in a finish, 'Heel' should be said with a *pleasurable* intonation, as if to say 'I'm pleased with what you have just done; now you can finish to heel'.

With fast pace in heelwork, 'Heel' can be given with a *slightly excitable* intonation, as in 'Watch now, we are going to heel fast'. With slow pace, 'Heel' can be said with a *deep* and very slightly slower tone, as if to say 'Watch now, tread carefully'.

Well, that's ten different tones for the one word 'Heel'! You can convey so much more with that one word if the right intonation is used. It will teach your dog to recognise what you require in a particular situation and to respond appropriately.

advanced stand, sit and down

Another exercise that can be included in advanced heelwork is the advanced stand, sit and down. It is one of the exercises in the British obedience Test 'C'. Walking at heel, the dog is commanded to stand while the handler keeps walking. The handler may walk around in a square, or by another route, and pick the dog up with the command 'Heel'; then the same thing is done with the other two positions, the sit and the down. The three positions are not always in that order.

When teaching this new dimension in heelwork, it is best to follow up each of the commands with 'Stay' and to stop only for about a second. As progress is made and your dog learns to recognise what the exercise is all about, you can gradually leave out the 'Stay' and cease stopping for even a fraction of a second. Keep your eyes on your dog, ensure that it obeys instantly and don't allow it to creep forward.

reinforcing the stays

When dogs have reached a certain standard in training and gradually start doing more advanced work, it is a very good idea to reinforce the stays.

With your dog on the leash, tell it to stay and turn around to face it so that you are nearly the length of the leash away. Say 'Stay' again, at the same time holding up the palm of your right hand as a signal to stay, and pulling very gently on the leash with your left hand; three gentle pulls are quite enough. Then relax and repeat. Relax once more and repeat again. Relax, return to your dog. Praise and dismiss. Although you have given the initial command to the dog to stay, it is necessary to repeat it each time, just as you are about to tempt the dog to move with the gentle tugs on the leash. The dog has to resist these temptations to move, and you are therefore reinforcing the training. As time goes on the tugs can gradually be made stronger. You need to be in direct line with the dog's body, so that it can use its weight to resist your pull. The exercise can later be done from other angles, but then the pulls should be very light or you will pull the dog over! Much depends on the breed and structure of the dog. For example, a Rottweiler is a broad, heavy dog that needs a fair bit to shift it, whereas the Saluki is a very slim, light dog that can be made to topple over quite easily.

I once showed this reinforcing to a group of instructors in a club in South Australia. A few years later I was told that one of the instructors, taking an advanced class, showed his handlers how to do it a week after I had visited them. Well, the results were excellent. He finished by saying to his class, 'In case you are wondering what we call this aspect of dog training, it is called "concreting".' Highly amused, his fellow instructors let him go on using the word for months, until someone eventually took pity and corrected him.

stays out of sight

Before you train your dog to stay while you go out of sight, it must be reliable at staying when you are in sight.

When an instructor feels that the dogs are ready for this, the class should be taken close to something behind which they can hide, and preferably something through which each dog can partially see its handler and the handler can keep an eye on the dog. A thinnish hedge, bushy shrubs or a few parked cars might be ideal. The reason for not going too far away is that if any of the dogs does move, the handler must be able to take it back to the original position as quickly as possible. Also, handlers should keep reappearing in the early days of this new exercise. It gives confidence to the dogs who need it, and it impresses upon the clever dog, who may have intentions of nicking off, that you are still keeping a very close watch on it.

As the days and weeks pass you can start to hide behind something more solid, and for longer periods. But vary the periods, keeping the dog guessing as to when you could return. Once your dog is quite happy to be left for a while, and you feel confident that it will stay, you can start extending the distance you walk to go out of sight.

In a class situation, an instructor may have dogs who are at various stages of doing the stays: a few might still be doing them on the leash. But it is quite easy to teach all the dogs at the same time. The instructor can say something like this:

'Handlers, we will now do a sit-stay, or a drop-stay, but since your dogs are all at various stages of training in these stay exercises, I shall leave it up to each of you when to return to your dog. When you have done so, pause for a moment. Praise it quietly, and heel it away quietly by doing an immediate right-about turn (without even taking a step forward to do it) and when you have got right away from the class you can dismiss your dog. This way you won't be disturbing the other dogs.

'You will notice that I have assembled you over here in such a way that those who wish to go out of sight will have to walk only a few metres to hide behind those trees or parked cars. The reason why I asked you to do an about-turn to take your dog away from the class is so that you can convey to the dog that the stay can often be followed by heeling in the opposite direction from the one you were taking when you told it to stay. This method helps ensure that your dog will stay, and not creep forward as many dogs do. Dogs that creep forward are often those that, having completed the stay, are heeled forward, then praised. In other words they get to know from experience that the stay is followed by heeling forward, so they creep forward in anticipation. At this stage of training you don't have to praise your dog when you return to it. You can leave that until after you have about-turned and heeled it away from the class. When training alone during the week, you can use two more variations by doing an immediate right or left turn. So by using all of these turns you are impressing upon your dog a kind of imaginary line across in front of its front paws, over which you are not taking it and across which it must not creep.'

Over the years I have noticed that quite a number of handlers in Australia have difficulty with stays, especially stays out of sight. Yet I rarely noticed this problem during my years in England. Although this puzzled me at first, I came to the conclusion that the different conditions under which clubs in the two countries trained had a great bearing on the performance of the stays. Because of the colder climate in the British Isles, clubs train inside community halls a lot of the time and handlers don't have to go far to be out of sight— perhaps an adjoining room or passageway. It is an enclosed environment and most of the dogs remain relaxed; they cannot really run off anywhere. They all become conditioned to doing plenty of stays and consequently become very reliable even on outside training areas in the warmer weather.

By contrast, in Australia we train outside all year round, with wide-open spaces on which to train, and because of so much space there is a tendency for more heelwork to be done and not enough stays. To do stays out of sight, everyone usually has to walk a fair way to hide behind something suitable.

A few years ago my conclusions were confirmed by a young woman who came to see me with a slight problem she had with a dog. About two years earlier she had emigrated to Australia from New Zealand, where she had trained an obedience champion. She told me she had noticed that so many people had trouble with the stays in all the clubs she had seen in Australia, yet she had never witnessed that problem in all the years she trained in New Zealand. When we conferred in detail on this subject it became clear that, because of the cooler climate, the conditions clubs train under in New Zealand are similar to those in the British Isles. (Incidentally, obedience tests in New Zealand are virtually the same as in Great Britain and South Africa, whereas the obedience trials in Australia are more or less the same as in the United States. But that has nothing to do with the training of the dogs.) Anyway, I found it most interesting to discuss such matters with someone who had come from another country, and to learn that her observations coincided with mine.

So I strongly urge instructors to do more stays, to do more stays out of sight close to suitable hiding-places—and to find shady areas in which to do these during the hot weather.

16

agility and jumping tricks

In the past few years agility has become very popular, and more and more dog clubs and individual trainers and handlers are making their own equipment for this particular sport **(Fig. 34)**. It is amazing that it didn't start long before it did, because it is really nothing new. For many years, police-dog training centres have had obstacle courses comprising a large variety of jumps, ramps, ladders and tunnels.

The obstacle courses in those training centres have two purposes. Firstly, the dogs acquire the confidence to tackle all kinds of natural obstacles as they pursue offenders to secure their arrest. Secondly, the dogs enjoy the activity and it helps them to relax, especially after doing something mentally draining.

All that is really needed before you start teaching your dog agility work is basic obedience and common sense. Dogs should be at least eighteen months of age before they begin agility work because most of the obstacles to be jumped require a lot of physical effort and the dog's bones and muscles need to be fully developed.

But it is also essential that you have adequate control over your dog: it must come whenever called, and must not get over-excited to the degree that it might run off and possibly pick a fight with another dog—that is what can happen if a handler gets a dog too hyped up. You need to make it fun for your dog and at the same time do everything with care to avoid unnecessary accidents.

When you start, always train your dog on the simple obstacles first, and teach them separately. If the first obstacle is adjustable, set it at its lowest or shortest. Once the dog understands what you require, you can gradually increase the height or length. As with everything else in dog training, work with the dog on the leash until you are certain it knows what to do; then you can try it off the leash.

Those are the basic principles. Now let's make a start with the first jump. I think the first one a dog should be taught is the normal high jump that we use in obedience training and trials. Use just the baseboard first and take your dog over, by holding the leash in your left hand, about half a metre (18 in.) from the clip, so that you have your right hand perfectly free to entice and signal the dog to jump over as you say in a very enthusiastic voice 'Over!'

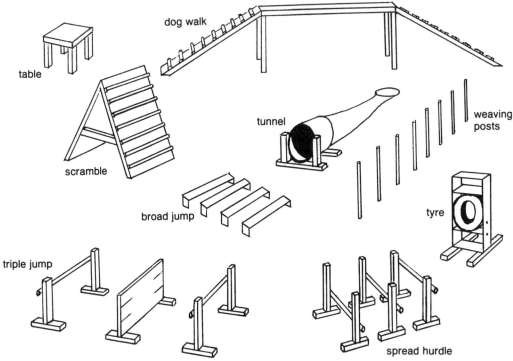

Fig. 34. Agility equipment.

and 'Good dog!'. Walk on a few paces, turn around and go over the jump again. Get that pattern established first in case you go in for obedience trials, where the dog will have to go over the jump, retrieve the dumbbell and return over the jump to you. When your dog understands the meaning of 'Over!' you can try it over a bar jump, set low to the ground to make it perfectly obvious to the dog that it cannot run underneath.

Now let's try teaching the dog to jump through a hoop—a car tyre in this case, set in an adjustable high jump. Before we start we should get the dog to walk through a tyre standing on the ground. Sit your dog facing the tyre. Pass the leash through it. Kneel down on the opposite side and

slightly to one side. Hold the top of the tyre steady with your left hand. Hold the leash short in your right hand, and have that hand in the centre of the tyre. Put your head down, so that you are looking at your dog and it is looking at you *through* the tyre. Invite him, 'Rufus, through!' and praise him. When the dog has got the idea, you can progress to the lowest height of the adjustable hoop set in the vertical stand.

When Rufus understands 'Through!' get him to walk through the drum part of the drum and tunnel. Once he really gets used to that, try the full tunnel stretched tight. Leave him at the entrance to the drum (you will need the assistance of someone to pull the tunnel tight, and of another person to hold your dog on a short leash), while you go around to the far end, crawl only half a metre into the tunnel and quietly call the dog through, with plenty of praise. Don't raise your voice in the tunnel as this can put him off. If your dog responds by straining to come to you through the tunnel, the person holding the leash should let go; if the dog tries to go around outside the tunnel, the leash-holder should not let go. The dog will learn by simple trial and error that it will be released only if it comes through the tunnel.

Once your dog enjoys running through the tunnel, you can get it to go through on command while you run along the outside and greet it with praise when it emerges from the far end. In subsequent stages the plastic tunnel can be slackened a bit more each time, so that the dog has to put its head down and push its way through.

The next obstacle is the table, which is adjustable for height. This should present no problem if you have taught your dog to jump up onto a table to be groomed. Pat the tabletop with your right hand a couple of times and say with great gusto 'Up!', praise your dog, then tell it to drop on the table for a while; praise and dismiss it.

When you know that your dog likes going up on the table, try walking it off the table by leading it down a little ramp, then up the ramp again. Walk it up and down on your left a few times, on the leash. You could quite easily use the command 'Heel' at this stage on the leash. Later, when your dog knows what is required and is doing it off the leash, all you need to say is 'Up!' and it will do the rest.

When your dog is very confident about going up the ramp, you can train it on the ramp-and-bridge obstacle, known as the 'dog walk'. Once again on the leash, move your dog slowly up the ramp, so that you are still close beside it; then along the bridge and all the way down the ramp at the other end without letting it leap off before it gets to the end.

To get the dog to go over the scramble, a steep A-frame ramp, it is best to begin by taking it up to the obstacle, encouraging it to put its front paws up the slope and praising it there for a while. Do that a few times. When you believe it is quite happy about that, make a short run at the obstacle so that the dog builds up some momentum to take it up to the top of the slope. You may not be tall enough to stretch your left hand, which holds the leash, up to the top, so have the table (at its low height) next to the scramble, and you will be able to step up onto it as you encourage your dog to go over the scramble and down the other side with plenty of praise.

Next we come to the upright poles through which your dog has to zig-zag as you walk along the right-hand side. You could start off with the dog sitting at heel so that the first pole is between you and your dog. Imagine that you have already zig-zagged through a few poles which are now behind you. As you step forward, beckon your dog over to you with the word 'In!' and allow it to come to the right of the second pole. Then say 'Out!' as you step forward and put your *left* foot up against the right-hand side of the third pole. As you do that, you can also indicate to the dog with the palm of your right hand, so that the back of your hand is against the left side of the pole, at the dog's eye-level. This will help to guide your dog around the left side of the pole. Then say 'In!' and allow the dog to come to the right of the fourth pole—and so on all the way through, praising on every response.

It is best to use a set of short poles when you start teaching this exercise. With a short leash in your left hand, you can walk along with your left arm over the top of the poles.

Finally we come to what is called the 'spread hurdle', which consists of three bar-jumps set at gradually increasing heights. Always start by getting your dog to jump over one, set at its lowest. Then get it to jump two by putting the next jump very close to the first and at the next height up. As you take your dog over a few times, it will learn by experience that there are two bars there—at different heights and one just beyond the other. Then you add the third bar close to the second. Once again your dog will see that there are three there, and will learn that it has to jump higher and further to clear all three. As time goes on these bars can be set very gradually higher and further apart, until your dog can jump the regulation measurement.

All the details of these agility obstacles, including all the measurements for large and small dogs, can be obtained from the controlling kennel club in your country (see Appendix, p. 143).

When you have taught your dog how to jump over, go through, and climb up and down all these obstacles separately, you can start putting them all together. Like everything else in training, it is quite easy if you take it step by step.

working without equipment

I can imagine a lot of people, who would like to teach their dogs to do all the things I've explained, declaring that they have neither the access to such equipment, nor the time, finance or knowhow to construct their own jumps and obstacles. Besides, even if they had the equipment, it would

all have to be transported, set up for a display, dismantled and taken home again whenever they were asked to put on a show. All that means a lot of hard work.

Well, I shall now show you how you can teach your dog to carry out many of the jumping tricks, and how you can put on a display with your dog, or with a small group of handlers and their dogs, without any equipment at all! Surprised? It is actually quite easy: you use yourself! You can teach your dog to jump over your leg, over your arm, to zig-zag through your legs as you walk along slowly, and to do many other things such as jumping up into your arms, and—if you can take the weight—jumping up onto your back.

The easiest jump to start with is over your leg. With your leash in your left hand, sit your dog beside a thick tree-trunk. Tell the dog to stay, take one pace forward, turn at right-angles to the left and face the tree. Place your left foot against the tree at about 30 centimetres (1 ft) above the ground. Give the command 'Over' in a joyful tone, and at the same time signal with your right hand in such a way as to encourage your dog to jump over your left leg, and praise it the instant it responds. It will not take long to learn this, especially if you have taught it to jump over, say, the first two boards of a high jump.

As progress is made during the next few days, you can place your left foot a little higher up the tree-trunk. Later you will be able to do it without the aid of a tree—which means you'll have to learn to balance on your right foot! Within a short time you will be able to do it without a leash, sitting your dog a few metres away so that it can make a run and leap over your leg.

An alternative way of teaching this is to

sit down on a box with your left leg lying horizontally across a high jump set low. Use the same command and signal with your right hand to encourage the dog to jump over your leg, under which are the high-jump boards. It is always good to try different methods, because what works with one dog just might not work with another.

The next exercise you can teach your dog is to jump over your arm. It is just a case of substituting your left arm for your left leg. Tell your dog to stay, step forward about 2 metres, turn to your left and go down on one knee. Outstretch your left arm horizontally, say 'Over', signal with your right hand for your dog to jump over your left arm, and praise it on response.

Perhaps the easiest way of teaching your dog to jump through your arms is to make a hoop out of a piece of hosepipe and get your dog to go through that first, as explained earlier in connection with walking through a rubber tyre: say 'Through' in an inviting way and lead the dog through the hoop on the leash, but use your right hand, as if you were still holding the leash, as a signalling hand to entice the dog through. As time goes on, raise the hoop a little higher every day, perhaps 5 centimetres (2 in.) at a time. Very soon your dog will be leaping through on command alone. This will enable you to hold the hoop with both hands. Over the next few days, put your hands further around the hoop until they nearly meet. By now your dog will be jumping not only through the hosepipe hoop but through your arms, also forming a hoop **(Fig. 35)**. Finally, get it to jump through your arms without the hoop.

When you call your dog from a few metres away to jump through your arms, it is a good idea to lean down and look

Fig. 35.   Jumping through a hoop. When the dog knows how to jump through a hoop you can put your arms progressively further around the hoop. Later the dog should jump through your arms without the hoop.

through your arms at it as you give the command; this attracts the dog. Just as it is about to jump through, get your head out of the way.

Dogs get to know the difference between the words 'Over' and 'Through'. Provided you use them appropriately, the dog will associate 'Over' with having to jump completely over the top of something, and 'Through' with having to go through something round or square.

Knowing what 'Through' means, the dog can now be taught how to jump

Fig. 36. Teaching the dog to jump through another hoop shape formed with left arm and thigh. Say 'Through' and beckon the dog through with your right hand. Praise on response.

through your arm and leg. This is not as hard as you might think. Once again, leave your dog in a sit-stay and take up your position a few metres ahead facing to the left. Balancing on your right foot, raise your left knee until the thigh is nearly horizontal. Bend your left elbow outwards as you just touch your left knee with the fingers of your left hand. You have now formed a hoop shape with your left arm and thigh. Say 'Through', beckon the dog through with your right hand and praise on response **(Fig. 36)**.

When your dog really understands this exercise, you can teach it to jump through your right leg and arm behind your back! It's a little harder to keep your balance when you do this, but it helps if you hold your right heel between the thumb and first finger of your right hand. As you say 'Through', you can flick the thumb and finger of your left hand behind your back, which will help to encourage the dog through.

I did say earlier that all these exercises can be done without having to transport, erect, use and dismantle a lot of equipment. But there are two small pieces of equipment, apart from a dumbbell, that I often carry when giving displays, and these are two light hoops made of plastic hosepipe. Having taught your dog to jump through one hoop, which was used purely as an aid to teaching it to jump through your arms, now get your dog to jump through two hoops held 5 to 8 centimetres (2–3 in.) apart. As time goes on widen the distance until they are about 30 centimetres (1 ft) apart. You can kneel down on one knee for this exercise, keeping the bottom of the hoops about 30 centimetres off the ground.

Another variation with the two hoops is to start off by having them together, and every day to twist them a little at a time until finally your dog will jump through crossed hoops. This act looks very impressive to any audience. It is a good idea to hold the crossed hoops at the two points where they cross, with the thumb and three fingers of your left hand above the dog as it jumps through and your right hand similarly underneath. Holding the hoops like this will prevent them slipping **(Fig. 37)**.

Now let's try something quite different: teaching your dog to zig-zag in and out of

Fig. 37. Jumping through crossed hoops. When teaching this trick, hold the hoops where they cross, with thumb and three fingers of the left hand above and similarly with the right hand underneath to prevent the hoops slipping.

your legs as you walk along slowly. As with some of the jumping exercises, you can use the command 'Through' with this exercise.

Start with your dog at heel sitting beside you. Now take one stride forward with your right foot and hold it there. Put your head down to your right side and say in an inviting tone 'Through', and at the same time flick the finger and thumb of your right hand down low, so that the noise attracts your dog to get up and move between your legs to your right hand. Praise upon response.

As the dog comes through step forward with your left foot and, putting your head down to your left, say 'Through' and entice it through your legs by flicking your left thumb and finger. You may have to assist your dog by physically guiding its head in the required direction with your other hand.

And so the process continues—to the right, then to the left, then right, then left, and so on. After about three times each way, say 'Heel' and your dog should sit at your left side as you come to a halt with your feet together.

As time goes on you will not have to use your hands so much in enticing and guiding your dog. After several weeks you won't have to keep saying 'Through' at every zig-zag; your dog should just obey the first command and carry out the habitual pattern. You will also be able to keep moving slowly once it really gets to know the procedure. But don't overdo it. I find that six walk-throughs are quite enough, i.e. three to the right and three to the left. You will discover that an audience finds it very amusing to watch and that the dogs seem to enjoy doing it. After all, dogs often do like to show off!

Another little trick you can perform, especially in front of a small group when you don't have much room, is a figure eight around your legs as you stand astride. I have found that this trick greatly amuses small children. It is based on the zig-zag and you can start by using the same command.

Firstly, have your dog at heel in the sit position. Now place your right foot to the right, say 'Through' and entice your dog across in front of you by flicking your left thumb and finger down at the dog's height. As the dog starts to come across you, attract it by flicking your right thumb and finger behind you to make it walk between your legs to your right hand. Give praise and continue to entice it with your right hand around your right leg to the front of you again. Then your left hand takes over behind you to entice the dog between your legs once more. Praise again and get it to follow your left hand around your left leg. That completes a circuit of a figure-eight pattern. You can do it once more without stopping, and then say 'Sit' as your dog comes to your left side. After doing this for a few days the dog should recognise what you require when you put

your right foot to the right. You can then replace the command 'Through' with the command 'Figure eight'.

To teach a dog to jump up into your arms needs a lot of skill and perfect timing, and you must also be strong enough to do it. Border Collies and Miniature Poodles are ideal for learning this trick: they are lightweight dogs and have a good spring action in their hind legs. I certainly would not recommend that anyone try it with a breed any larger than a German Shepherd.

Leave your dog in the sit position and stand about 2 metres in front, facing it. Now turn your whole body no more than 45° to your left. Stretch your right leg out in front of you and bend your left leg slightly. Bring your left forearm up horizontally. That is your preparation. Now give the command 'Up!' simultaneously patting the top of your chest rapidly three times with your right hand. As the dog runs to leap up, it has your right leg to run up. You have to be very quick to wrap your right arm underneath the dog's hindquarters, so that it does not fall as it rests its front legs at the knee-joints over your left forearm. Praise upon response and dismiss as you let it down. It is most important that you have your feet correctly placed. If you have them together, the impact of the dog jumping up into your arms could make you topple backwards.

If and when your dog can do this trick, you can also get it to jump up onto your back. Leave it in the sit position and stand with your back to it about 2 metres in front. Have one foot further forward than the other, and bend slightly at your knees as you lean your body forwards. Pat your back with the back of one of your hands as you say 'Up!'. As it leaps and you brace yourself for the impact, clasp your hands together, ensuring that your arms run down each side of your back, so that the dog's legs don't slip between your arms and your body. The moment you feel the dog land on your back, say 'Stay!'. Quietly praise and dismiss it.

It is most important that you have one foot placed further forward than the other so that you can brace yourself and maintain your balance. If you had your feet together and your dog jumped onto your back, you could easily fall flat on your face!

Another way of receiving your dog is to kneel down on one knee. When the dog has jumped onto your back you can slowly stand up and walk fowards, giving it a pick-a-back. Also, make sure the dog is hanging on to your shoulders with its front paws. You may need some assistance with this trick: the assistant could pat the top of your back to entice the dog up.

This type of training can be great fun for both dogs and handlers. It also provides great entertainment to those who watch, and who like to see dogs enjoying their work.

17

demonstration work

I think that some of the most enjoyable times handlers can have with their dogs are when they are working together in demonstration teams. This is so enjoyable because you can get out there and work your dogs in such a variety of ways, and use your voice as much as you like, and use your hands to assist your dogs, whereas you are not allowed to do these things in obedience competitions. Having that freedom, and knowing that your capable commentator on the microphone will smooth things over in a flash if anything unforeseen happens, helps the handlers to relax.

What do you need to form, organise and run a happy and enthusiastic demonstration team?

Well, first of all you need volunteers who have at least reached the stage where their dogs are doing some of the exercises off the leash. You will naturally need an instructor to train the team, and one or two team leaders for the handlers to follow in certain exercises. But most important of all, you must have a very capable commentator on the microphone. That person does not need to be a trainer or handler, but he or she must have the ability to speak confidently, quickly and concisely about the demonstration team and the

club it represents, and about dog training generally. The commentator also needs to be able to smooth things over if a dog should happen to do the wrong thing. This can often be done by offering some humorous explanation. The commentator needs to capture and hold the interest of the audience, regardless of its size; to know all about the exercises and tricks that are to be performed; and to know when (and how) to ask the audience to remain quiet and when to allow and encourage it to applaud.

Next, you need to have a rough plan of what you are going to do in your demonstrations, and to do this you will have to assess what the dogs are capable of doing and decide if any special equipment will be required. When all these things have been discussed, and everyone has a fairly good idea of what they are going to do, rehearsals should be held.

It is a good idea to time the rehearsals, because they often take longer than expected. Suggestions from the team should be welcomed and modifications made in order to streamline the whole programme. I believe an actual performance should last from twenty to thirty minutes, no longer, so in that time you have to get in as much work as possible. It must be kept moving with zip; you must keep the audience interested. If there are pauses, some members of the audience may drift away.

When a rehearsed team puts on a good demonstration, it is not only providing entertainment for the public; it is also showing people what can be done in dog training, and that everyone who owns a dog should be a responsible owner. At the same time it is publicising the work of that particular club and of obedience dog-training clubs in general.

The audiences will vary, depending mainly on the size and type of function. You may be invited to perform at a large agricultural show or at a small town carnival. Your demonstration team will also be welcomed at fetes, charity shows, and places such as nursing homes where patients really enjoy watching the dogs and meeting them afterwards.

Here are a few suggestions that a team might like to try out, and on which it can always introduce variations.

First of all, the demonstration team must march on, in one line or two, during which they can be introduced by the commentator. I think this introduction should be general: spectators are not really interested in excessive detail—they are anxious to see the dogs work.

The first item ought to be heelwork, because after all that is what the dogs are taught first. But this should not be for very long. It should be designed to include everything in heelwork, perhaps twice in some cases. It should also be performed to make it look neat, and spectacular. For example, if a team consists of six handlers and dogs walking abreast of each other, the team leader on the far left can drop his or her dog, then two steps on the next handler can do the same, and so on. When

they have all dropped their dogs in what has become a diagonal line, the handlers can walk on a little further, about-turn, walk straight through the dogs, all about-turn and, starting with the leader, heel their dogs one by one as they continue to walk in a straight line abreast of each other. When walking like this it is best that they should dress by the left—which means they should be glancing to the left to keep in line with the leader. At the same time they can also glance down to the left to watch their dogs. The staggered walking drop looks more impressive than an ordinary drop where handlers do it all together as they halt. If you have two teams of six or more facing each other, you can do counter-marching, which also looks impressive. Stands, sits or drops can also be included, just at the point where both teams are in line with each other.

Another way of demonstrating some impressive heelwork is to have them all going around in a huge figure eight, crossing each other in the centre, just as you would see in a motorcycle display team. Perhaps the easiest and quickest way of doing this is to have two teams of, say, eight, walking side by side. The two leaders gradually turn away from each other to form two circles, i.e. the leader on the right goes around in a circle clockwise, and the leader on the left goes anti-clockwise. When the two leaders meet again, one crosses over in front of the other, and with the handlers continuing to follow their respective leaders, everyone is soon heeling in a figure eight, which looks most impressive. When the leaders come together again, they can straighten out with their teams following them, and they will soon be formed in two straight lines again.

The recall can be demonstrated in many

ways. One way is for the whole team, heeling in a large circle clockwise, to turn right and immediately to halt. Handlers leave their dogs, march to the centre of the circle, about-turn and halt. Then one after the other the dogs are recalled. All finish together. The recall can be done again: the handlers leave their dogs to walk to the outer circle, about-turn, halt and call them one after the other.

The recall using hand-signals only can be simply demonstrated with three dogs in the centre of the arena. Two can be signalled to come in one direction, and the third to come between the other two from the opposite direction. Meanwhile other members of the team can be demonstrating a sit and/or drop-stays. By showing three different exercises at once, a lot of time can be saved.

I well remember being in a team of eight on one occasion, when we took up positions representing the eight points of a Union Jack. We each left our dog and stood by the dog opposite, and then signalled our dogs to come. They all came, passing each other in the centre in the best British tradition! You have to have some very sound dogs for that. You certainly can not afford to have a scrap in the middle!

Retrieves by four dogs simultaneously can look very effective if the handlers stand in the centre facing outwards to the four corners of the ring.

Stand for examination can be shown in a large circle, where every handler leaves his or her dog and examines the dog in front. That way each dog is watching its own handler, and vice versa. While this is being observed by the audience, the commentator can assure the spectators that the dogs are trustworthy, and can invite a few children into the ring to meet perhaps

two or three selected dogs, which are then taken into the centre of the ring. The handlers should show the children how to let the dogs sniff the backs of their hands first, and then stroke the dogs gently. The commentator can meanwhile describe it all for the audience.

Audiences will vary. One day not long ago, we put on a demonstration during Open Day at an animal farm for children. There were all kinds of animals there—sheep, goats, calves, ponies, rabbits, just about everything you could think of. Well, when our commentator suggested that any child who might like to come into the demonstration ring to meet and stroke the dogs could do so, we were inundated with children. Within seconds there were more people inside the ring than outside it. We couldn't believe it at first, but it wasn't surprising really: all the children there that day were extremely well oriented towards animals.

When you have demonstrated all these basic obedience exercises, you should move on to the jumping exercises and tricks outlined in the previous chapter; these are based on obedience as well. And it doesn't matter if you don't have equipment of the type used in agility or obedience trials. You can get a dog to retrieve a dumbbell by jumping over the back of a dog in the stand position and returning. You can do a novel recall by calling a small dog like a Miniature Poodle under a large dog like an Irish Wolfhound in the stand position. In our club's team our two leaders work a brace of German Shepherd dogs and a brace of Scotch Collies. When they stand close side by side facing in opposite directions, I get my own Shepherd to leap right over them. This shows several things at once: that all four dogs will stand close together, that they will stay there, and that they show no signs of fear or distraction as another dog jumps over them.

Whenever possible I like to get a few children from the audience involved in our demonstrations by asking them if they would like to help with some jumping tricks. So just before the display I show them how my dog will jump through and over my arms. The children are always thrilled to see this and are very eager to try it. I ask two of them to hold hands to form a hoop while my dog jumps through. Then I ask them to keep holding hands and to kneel down on one knee facing each other, and I get my dog to jump over their arms, which are held horizontally. Then I ask two more children to kneel down beside them to do the same, so that the dog has four pairs of arms to jump over. (The most she has leapt over is eight pairs of arms.) In preparing this, I always tell the children to lean back slightly and keep their heads back to give the dog plenty of room to jump. I have done a similar jump by asking five or six children to lie face-downwards close together on a carpet. When all are quite still, I get my dog to leap right over them as if jumping over a broad jump. The children think this is great fun (as do the dogs) and love being able to take part.

From a time standpoint, demonstration work suits a lot of handlers, especially those who have a limited amount of spare time. You only need to arrive about ten or fifteen minutes before the actual display (perhaps earlier if you have to set up equipment), do the performance, and be prepared to talk to spectators afterwards for a while, because they like to ask about the dogs and to meet them. After that you can go home when you please. It is quite different from an obedience trial or dog show, where you are committed to attend virtually all day. But it all depends on where your interests lie.

Some demonstration teams like to wear a uniform displaying the club badge and I think that is to be commended; but I don't think it is essential. It's what you put into the demonstration which really counts. Years ago I saw a dog club put on a demonstration in which handlers' uniforms were immaculate. Unfortunately, at least three-quarters of the time was taken up with repetitive heelwork and stays. Two dogs did separate recalls and two did separate retrieves. And that was it. The spectators were bored stiff and so was I. Later, another team of handlers, all dressed in different clothes, put on a marvellous demonstration with many different things in it. Their work captivated the audience, which expressed its appreciation accordingly.

Sometimes teams will have dogs that have reached different stages of training. This should present no problem at all, if you make use of what the beginners can do, and put the more experienced dogs through other exercises. For example, a stay or a recall may be required in a group where two handlers can do the exercise only on the leash. Those two can do it that way and return to their dogs earlier than the others if they please, and be allowed to call their dogs first in the case of the recall. The commentator can explain that these two dogs have been trained for only a short time whereas the rest of the team has been working together for quite a while. This gives the spectators an idea of how the dogs are trained, and reminds them that it is not all taught by magic—only some of it is!

18

scent work

I always think scent work is the most fascinating aspect of dog training. Today there are many different fields in which dogs are working with their number-one sense—the sense of smell. More and more dogs in the services are being trained to detect narcotics, and others to sniff out explosives. There seems to be no limit to what we can train dogs to find, and in so doing we can learn much from them. In fact, the dog will always know more about scent work than we ever will.

I would like to confine this chapter to the basics that instructors and handlers need to follow in training dogs to retrieve articles in the seek-back and scent-discrimination exercises. These exercises are found in the more advanced obedience tests and trials, but you can have a lot of fun just doing them at home or in demonstrations. The prerequisite is that the dog be able to retrieve.

Prior to teaching scent work to the class, the instructor could recommend that when handlers do retrieves during the coming week, they leave the dog in the sit position and go forward and hide the article behind a piece of furniture or (if outdoors) behind something in the garden or yard. While the article is being hidden mysteriously, the dog should be watching,

so that it will have a reasonable idea where to look. On returning to stand beside the dog, the handler only needs to place the right hand lightly over its nose for two to three seconds and say in a quiet drawn-out way 'Find!' or 'Seek!' and the dog should go off to find and retrieve what has been hidden.

At the next training session at the dog club, the instructor can start showing the class how to do a seek forward before doing a seek back.

seek forward

This should be the first exercise of the day. A large piece of fresh ground, on which a lot of people have not walked recently, should be chosen.

The instructor should ask a handler to sit his or her dog and, having told it to stay, leave it and walk forward about twenty paces, place the small article in the grass and return to the dog on exactly the same track. The handler should then give the dog the scent and, at the same time as saying 'Find!' or 'Seek!', should beckon down with the right hand along the ground in the direction of the track. In time this will help the dog to understand three things: (1) to take the scent; (2) to track along the scent; and (3) to find the article bearing the scent.

The instructor should stand to one side so as to be able to give instruction to the handler and talk to the rest of the class, which might be assembled in a relaxed group several paces behind and slightly to one side of the handler **(Fig. 38)**. The next handler can do a seek forward a few metres away and parallel to the first. If there is any wind, the articles should be placed downwind (in the direction the wind is going) so that the dog is more likely to put its nose to the ground to follow the track. If the article is placed upwind (with the wind coming towards the dog), the dog will more than likely wind-scent the article, go straight to it and retrieve it all right, but will probably disregard the actual track, which has been impregnated twice by the handler going out and returning on it. The instructor must therefore check the direction of the wind and choose an area large enough to cater for all the handlers who wish to do a seek forward separately and parallel to each other. This means that the group should gradually shift down as each handler does it.

The following week the instructor can show the handlers how to do a seek back—provided their dogs are performing quite well in the seek forward.

seek back

Once again the instructor should check the direction of the wind, if any, on an area of training ground large enough for all the dogs to work in turn. Because this exercise follows on automatically, there is no real need for the instructor to give a brief explanation or demonstration. These can be given as each handler does the exercise.

With the group of handlers watching, the instructor can ask the first handler (this could be the handler who patiently waited to be the last the week before) to walk forward, with dog at heel, into the wind. After about a dozen paces, the instructor should ask the handler to drop the article discreetly while walking. When they have walked on another twenty paces or so, they can right-about turn and halt. The dog can then be given the scent and told to find. From that position the dog will be tracking downwind along the single track made by the handler. It must be realised that there is also the track made by the dog close and parallel to the handler's track. I believe this helps in the early days when teaching this exercise. The dog gets to know that, when given the command to find or seek, there is something to be found that bears the handler's scent somewhere back along that track. Later, turns can be very gradually introduced and the track itself very gradually lengthened.

So to recap on these two exercises. In the seek forward the human scent is being laid twice, i.e. going out and coming back. In the seek back the human scent is laid only once and the scent of the dog is parallel and close to it; they are in fact mingled together.

Later, a seek back can be done without the dog being in close company with the handler. The dog could be a fair distance away, having a free run. When the handler calls the dog to heel and gives it the scent to seek back, the dog will have only one scent to follow on the track, that of its handler.

Instructors should always advise handlers to use different articles each time, so that the dog will learn to find any article regardless of what shape it is and what it is

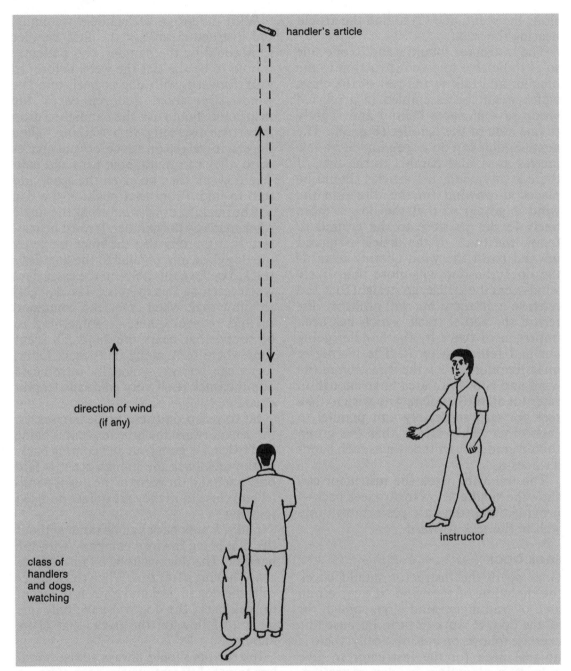

handler's article

direction of wind
(if any)

instructor

class of
handlers
and dogs,
watching

Fig. 38.   Seek forward. Having left the dog in a sit-stay, the handler walks downwind about 20 paces, places the article in the grass and returns to the dog by the same route. Note the position of the instructor, who can watch the dog, instruct the handler and describe everything to the class assembled in a group.

made of. If the same article is used every time, the dog will get to know what it looks like, and will also learn that, apart from the handler's scent, the article bears the dog's scent from its own saliva.

scent discrimination

When a dog has learnt how to do a seek forward and a seek back, scent discrimination is quite easy; but there are some differences and therefore we need to use a slightly different system in teaching this exercise. I think the best and most simple way of doing it is to get the dog to find an article belonging to the handler which has been placed at the end of a line of other articles.

The instructor can organise this exercise by asking for several articles that bear different human scents and placing them in a row a few metres away and across in front of the class. The articles, which might include a wallet, a glove, a bunch of keys, a pencil, an old shoe and a sock, should be placed about 60 centimetres (2 ft) apart in a straight line **(Fig. 39)**. The handler should take up a position about 2 metres from the first article in line with

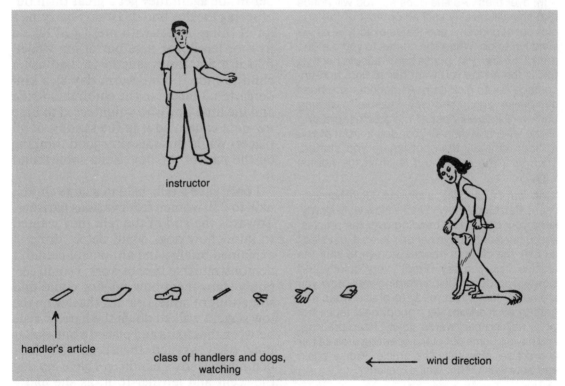

instructor

handler's article

class of handlers and dogs, watching

wind direction

Fig. 39. Scent discrimination. Articles bearing different human scents can be placed a short distance apart in a straight line with the handler's article placed at the far end. Having given the scent to the dog, the handler should stroll along the line of articles, with the dog on the leash, allowing it to sniff each one. When the dog sniffs its handler's article it should be encouraged to retrieve it to the handler, who should then walk backwards out of the scenting area to the spot where the dog was given the scent. Note the position of the instructor, the class and the direction of the wind, if any.

the rest and facing downwind. The instructor should then take the handler's article and place it at the end of the line.

When all this has been set up the instructor can explain to the handler and the class exactly what is required:

'Pat, with your dog sitting beside you, I want you to hold your leash in your left hand about half a metre away from the clip. When you give your Border Collie the scent with your right hand and say "Find!", and beckon the dog to go towards the line of articles, stroll along the side of the articles so that your dog, which is not really at heel but just strolling beside you, will be treading right over them. As she does so, you will notice that she will quickly sniff all or most of the articles out of curiosity, and that is exactly what we want her to do. When she comes to yours at the end of the line, Pat, praise her to assure her that this is the article you want her to find, and encourage her to pick it up. As soon as she does so, praise again and say "Come!", walking backwards slowly past all the articles, praising all the time, and then sit your dog in front of you at approximately the spot where you started. Then take the article and finish in the normal way.

'Now watch carefully, everyone. Give her your scent, Pat. Good, now "Find!". Now walk slowly, keep your dog in line treading over the articles, keep your leash above her and keep it just slack so that she can put her head down to sniff the articles. You can say "Find!" very quietly and slowly. The dog is discriminating well, now you are nearly there. Get ready to praise when she gets to your article. Very good; now recall her while walking backwards slowly, keep praising, and having come out of the scenting area sit her and praise. Now take the article. Praise again and now finish. That was excellent!

'Well now, handlers, you all had a good view of that, didn't you? You could see how Pat's dog methodically sniffed each article as they both moved along slowly. With perfect timing the dog was reassured with praise that this was the article required to be found, picked up and retrieved. As time goes on your dogs will be able to do this off the lead and you won't have to walk beside them. Remaining at the starting position, all you do is give the dog the scent, tell it "Find!" and watch it do the rest. You have three major exercises in this: the retrieve, the use of the nose, and the recall.'

You can have a lot of fun with your dog when you have taught it to retrieve and use its nose. I know I have. In my talks to schools I usually ask one of the children to hide something of mine in the classroom while I take my dog outside. When I bring her inside again they get a great thrill out of seeing the dog find it. To save carrying a lot of things about with me, I just take a five- or ten-dollar note out of my wallet, fold it a few times lengthwise and ask a child to hide it. One warm day at a kindergarten, I talked to the children outside and the little boy who volunteered to hide my note concealed it in the sandpit of all places. While this was very good thinking on the part of the boy, Zena soon found it.

I once gave a talk, held in a large church hall, to 250 women from various parishes. Towards the end of the talk they wanted to know how dogs could detect drugs. I explained briefly, and although I couldn't demonstrate that type of work, I could certainly show them how my dog could find something of mine. Leaving the dog on the low stage, I walked down the narrow aisle between the chairs and placed a one-dollar note (they existed then!) on the floor behind one lady's handbag. I gave my dog the scent and left her to it, as she had a large area to cover. Now I didn't notice at the time, but there happened to be a low coffee-table next to the closed door where they had been selling some cookery books before I arrived, and on the table next to these books was a large church collection plate full of money. My Border Collie went over to sniff it for a moment, and then (would you believe it) pulled out a ten-dollar note and brought it to me! Everyone including our local vicar roared with laughter. While part of me felt most embarrassed about my dog stealing ten dollars out of the collection plate, another part of me was seeking a logical reason why the dog had done this. Many thoughts flashed through my mind as the audience laughed. Had I had that very note in my possession? Had I possibly exchanged it with someone earlier? No, on both counts. Had I been to the local shops that day or the day before and passed that note across the counter, so that it was later given in change to a lady purchasing one of those recipe books? No, I hadn't been to the shops for at least two days. Then, as the laughter died down, I suddenly realised that, although for about three years I'd been getting my dog to find notes of mine,

this was the first occasion when other money had been present. That gave me the clue to what I had, unintentionally, been teaching her. Every Australian note, regardless of its denomination, has two scents on it: the smell of the paper, and that of the ink used in printing. It doesn't matter how many people handle a note; it still carries the smell common to all notes. So while I had been training my dog to find a banknote with my scent on it, she had picked up the idea that she should find something that had the smell of a banknote.

I was then able to explain why my dog had craftily tried to slip me the ten dollars. I took it from her but did not praise her: I sent her off again, and within half a minute she had found and retrieved my one-dollar note from behind the lady's handbag, for which I gave her plenty of praise. The last thought that ran through my mind that day was: 'I could make a lot of money out of this!'

19

tracking

Having, I hope, whetted your appetite with what I have had to say in the last chapter, I would now like to take the subject of scent work one huge step further, into the field of tracking. You don't need much space to teach a dog to do seek forward and later seek back, and even less room to do scent discrimination, but in tracking you are going to walk long distances and cover large areas, over different types of terrain and vegetation in a variety of weather conditions.

Tracking is a fascinating subject, and there is so much to learn about it. The main difference between general obedience and scent work is that in obedience our dogs are learning everything from us, whereas in scent work we are really learning from them, even though we have to use a certain amount of control.

There seems to be a growing interest in tracking in many countries, and although numerous articles have been written about it, most of which appear in canine magazines, there have been comparatively few books specifically on tracking. My main aim here is to help instructors and handlers make a start by explaining the theory of scent, how to lay tracks, how to control the dog, how to handle the tracking line, how weather conditions can affect the tracks, and so on. There is so much to learn.

Because scent work is such a wide and complex subject, I believe that it is best for all interested instructors, handlers and observers to attend a lecture before they are shown any of the practical work.

When handlers who wish to attend my tracking courses ask me what prerequisites they and their dogs need to have, I tell them that as long as they have taught their dogs basic obedience—i.e. heel, sit, down, stay and come—they have all they need. They do not need a CD (Companion Dog) title. It will be very useful if the dog can retrieve, but it is not essential: a dog can be trained to be an excellent tracker without ever retrieving.

I also point out that the objective of the short tracking courses I conduct is to teach the basic steps in tracking, but not necessarily to train handlers and dogs for tracking trials. As with obedience training, handlers need to know the basics first and these must be taught really well. There should be no margin for silly errors. When the basics have been learnt by both handler and dog, and the handler then has a strong desire to train for and enter tracking trials, I would certainly encourage them to do so.

The only equipment a handler needs for tracking is a suitable body-harness for the dog and a strong tracking line no less than 10 metres (33 ft) long. Beyond this, all you need is a dog with a good nose and a handler with a keen pair of eyes!

Having welcomed everybody to the tracking lecture, I always start by explaining very briefly and very simply the theory of scent. Fundamentally, scent is conveyed in two ways: by ground scent, and by wind scent.

ground scent

Basically, when you walk across a paddock, or anywhere else for that matter, you walk through a corridor of air. In the process, that air becomes very finely scented by you. In a very short time the scent will fall to the ground, laying a trail as it does so.

Besides the natural human scent, there will also be additional scents. There will be the scents of different types of *clothing* worn: wool, cotton, silk and many other materials have their own peculiar scents. There will also be the scents of the *footwear*, be it rubber gumboots, leather shoes or shoes made from other materials. Furthermore, people carry scents relating to their occupation, and these become ingrained to various degrees in the pores of the skin; no amount of washing will remove them. Even the soap and cosmetics we use have their own scents. You can go on and on. So when all those scents fall collectively to the ground, it is not all that hard for a dog with a good nose to track along that trail.

Now let us look at the ground. What has happened to it as the person has walked on it? Well, first of all the soil has been disturbed and that in itself will produce a scent. Secondly, the vegetation has been crushed, which also produces a scent—you only have to smell a recently cut lawn to know that. Thirdly, some insect life will unavoidably have been squashed, once again producing an odour that a dog can detect. So you can see what a lot of scents a trail can contain.

wind scent

This is the scent which is carried through the air by the wind from a human being, an animal or, to a lesser extent, an object that has been handled by a human or an animal.

In the case of an object with human scent on it (which I talked about in the last chapter), or indeed the actual track with human scent on it, I like to use the descriptive term *passive scent*. This means that human scent was put on that object or track by a person who has since gone completely away. It is interesting to note that whereas a dog can wind-scent an article which is a few metres away, it can wind-scent a living person who is several hundred metres away! I like to describe that as a *live scent*. It is a very strong scent, because it is being continuously emitted by the person and conveyed to the dog by the wind.

the basic procedure

When a track is to be laid by a person to whom I shall henceforth refer as the track-layer, he or she must first check the direction of the wind and lay the track downwind—which means that the wind should be against the track-layer's back. While describing what the track-layer has to do (as outlined below), I always illustrate on a board or on large cards by putting in the direction of the wind, then the starting peg, then the spot just beyond it

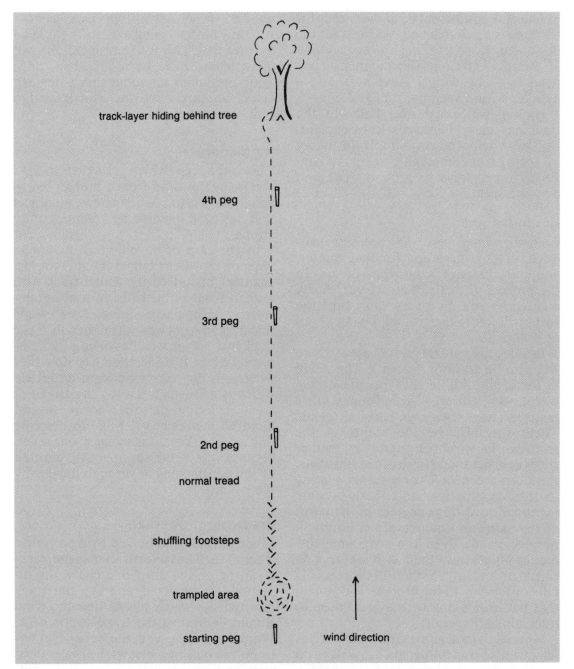

Fig. 40. A simple straight track, laid downwind. The track-layer tramples around on the ground one step beyond the starting peg. Shuffling footsteps are then made for a short distance, followed by a normal tread, with three more pegs inserted at intervals. Finally the track-layer can hide behind a thick tree.

where the track-layer will trample, then the shuffling footsteps, then the normal footsteps, then more pegs at intervals en route, and finally the tree behind which the track-layer will hide (**Fig. 40**). It is good if the track-layer is well known to the dog—another member of the family, for example. If this is not the case, the track-layer should make every attempt to get to know the dog, and make a fuss of it, just prior to laying the track.

The handler should have the dog on the leash at the left side, watching the track-layer go forward a few metres and insert a peg into the ground to mark the start of the track. The track-layer should then stand one step beyond the peg and trample around on the ground to create a good scent at the start, all the while talking to the dog to capture its attention. Then the track-layer should proceed downwind in a straight line with shuffling footsteps, to really disturb the vegetation and ground for the next few metres, but after that should adopt a normal tread, inserting three more pegs in the straight track at intervals of between 20 and 30 metres, and finally hiding behind something like a thick tree-trunk. It is very important for the handler to watch exactly where the track-layer has walked. The pegs used, during the early stages of tracking, are there for the handler's guidance.

It is also important that the handler have the dog under control and sitting at heel. The harness can then be put on the dog. The handler should stand the dog to buckle up the harness, roll out the tracking line behind them and clip it on to the harness. The leash and collar should be removed and carried either across the handler's shoulder or in a suitable pocket. During this preparation, the dog should remain quite still. Holding the tracking line about 25 centimeters (1 ft) from the clip, the handler should stroll up to the starting peg with the dog, not strictly to heel, and allow it to sniff the ground on which the track-layer has trampled. The handler should try to keep just behind the starting peg, and, with a beckoning right-hand signal close to the ground, say in a slow, quiet, coaxing way 'Find'. Often a dog will sniff around the trampled area for a few moments before following the scent along the track-layer's path.

As the dog proceeds, the handler should allow the tracking line to run through the left hand, and as it does so should raise that hand so that the line does not fall below the height of the dog. When the dog has proceeded forward a distance of 2 to 3 metres, the handler should grasp the line and follow behind the dog at the same speed, maintaining a comfortable tension on the line, the rest of which is trailing behind on the grass.

If the dog tracks consistently, it is not necessary for the handler to talk to it—it's best to allow it to get on with its work. Some dogs, if spoken to, will stop, return to their handlers for attention and forget all about the tracks. So the handler should use vocal encouragement only if this is necessary.

Handlers should not be surprised if their dogs pause for a moment to sniff the tops of the pegs before proceeding to track again. This is only natural because the track-layer will have had to exert hand pressure to insert the pegs, leaving a concentration of human scent there.

When the dog has only a few metres to go before it finds the track-layer behind the tree-trunk, the handler can afford to let more line run through the left hand. This gives the dog the opportunity of really going further out away from the handler in order to find the hidden track-layer.

As soon as the dog has found the track-layer, both track-layer and handler should praise it. After this, the handler should put the dog back on the slip-collar and leash, and remove the harness.

Within a very short time a dog will associate the putting on of its harness with tracking; in other words, it will know that it is now on duty. When the harness is taken off, it will know that the work is finished and that it is off duty. This association of ideas is the same with all working dogs who work in harness—for example, police dogs tracking, guide dogs leading the blind, dogs that pull sledges, and so on.

All this work can be explained, and some of it demonstrated, during the lecture. The plan of the tracks, the wind directions and how the dogs will work the tracks can be shown on a blackboard or whiteboard, or on large sheets of white paper on a board and easel. The way the track-layer places a peg, stands beyond it, tramples the ground and starts laying a track can be demonstrated in the lecture room. The way the handler should take the dog to the start can also be shown. In this case, an imaginary dog can be used at first and then, from the starting peg onwards, its place can be taken by one of the other handlers, who can hold the clip part of the tracking line close to the ground (imagining it to be a Dachshund tracking!). The handler can move slowly along the track (across the lecture room) as the instructor shows the class how the line should be allowed to run through the left hand, which then grips it at the required length, and how to follow behind the imaginary

dog, controlling it at a constant speed and keeping the required tension on the line.

recasting a dog

A very important point to teach is how to recast a dog if, for any reason, it loses the track. This can and should be demonstrated in the lecture room. It should be shown in slowmotion first so that everyone can fully grasp what is required.

Imagine your dog is tracking well and is leading out in front of you on a length of line about 5 metres long. Suddenly you realise that it has lost the track, or is confused in some way and finding it hard to continue. The first thing you must do is stop. You know for sure that your dog was on track to a point about 2 metres in front of where you have stopped. Call it to heel and then beckon it to pick up the track again. Often it will, and you can proceed. But when you recast your dog you must ensure that it does not get its legs tangled in the tracking line; so keep your left hand, which has been holding the line, above your head and pull the free end of the line down through it with your right hand (**Fig. 41**). Thus, as the dog is returning to you and possibly behind your back, the line is being drawn back through your left hand. This will ensure that the piece of line from your left hand to the dog (the piece you have been working your dog on) will not dangle down and get caught in its legs. Handlers cannot afford to have any unnecessary hold-ups in tracking; if they do, the continuity is broken, and that can cause confusion and sometimes failure.

So with the aid of a member of the class taking the part of a dog that has to be recast, I would ask the 'dog' to return to my heel in slowmotion, and everyone could see how I manipulate the line. Having done this twice in slowmotion I would

Fig. 41.   Recasting a dog in tracking. To ensure that the dog does not get its legs tangled in the tracking line, the handler should hold the line with the left hand above head height and pull the free end down through it with the right hand.

ask the person to return to my heel much faster, the way some fast, keen dogs do. This time the class could see how quickly I pull the line through my left hand.

other problems

I also believe it is necessary to show the class what can happen if the handler does not manipulate the leash properly; and how the dog can get out of control by running around its handler, who then becomes entwined in the tracking line—much to the amusement of the class! Sometimes a comical demonstration like this goes down very well. While the handlers have a good laugh, they are learning how important it is to do things calmly, methodically and with accuracy.

When handlers have a good idea of how a straight track should be laid and how the dog should be worked on it, a further plan should be drawn on the board which shows what will happen if the wind has changed direction, in this case to the right. As the track-layer walks straight the natural scent from his or her body is blown to the right and descends upon the ground more or less parallel to the trodden track. Soon after starting to track the dog is more than likely to divert to the right and track along where the human scent has fallen. If the dog walks consistently like that, it should be allowed to do so. Much depends on the strength of the wind: the stronger it is, the further away to the right the dog will track. At the end of the track the dog is likely to go past the track-layer, but will then suddenly wind-scent that person by lifting up its nose and, turning acutely to the left, will proceed straight to the track-layer **(Fig. 42)**.

turns

After the straight track has been shown on the board, more diagrams of tracks and how they can be affected by the wind should be drawn, so that the class can learn more and get an idea of what they will be doing in subsequent weeks. The next diagrams involve turns. As with everything in training, it is always best to start off gradually. I like to start with 45° turns, and then gradually progress to 90° turns.

This time we will imagine there is no wind. After the track-layer has inserted the first and second pegs, the third can be inserted at an angle so that it will indicate to the handler that there is a change of direction, in this case 45° to the right. When the track-layer has proceeded for another 10 to 15 metres, the fourth peg can be inserted at an angle to the left and pointing to, say, something like a bush behind which the track-layer can hide **(Fig. 43)**. When a track of this nature is composed of three straight lines, it is said to have three legs.

As the dog approaches the turns, the handler should watch very carefully to ensure that it does not go too fast and overshoot. So the handler must control the speed. It is important that when the dog turns to the right the handler should step around to the left in order to keep the tracking line in line with the dog's body; otherwise, if the dog feels a pull on its harness to its right, it is likely to pull in the opposite direction and go off the track. Conversely, the handler ought to step around to the right when the dog does a turn to the left. In time handlers get used

to this whenever they see their dogs negotiate turns, and they also learn to avoid a hard tension on the line at those times **(Fig. 44)**.

Provided the handler and dog have mastered the 45° turns in their practical work, right-angled turns can be introduced. In the next diagram we will imagine that there is a moderate breeze and the first leg of the track is laid downwind; but when the track-layer walks across wind on the second leg, the scent is blown to the left of that leg until the 90° angled turn to the left is made. The track-layer then proceeds downwind on the third leg to hide behind a parked car.

With this track you can expect the dog to track straight along the first and third legs; but it is likely to track parallel to the left of the second leg **(Fig. 45)**.

longer tracks

Another diagram can be drawn on the board to show handlers what they are likely to encounter with longer tracks in the future **(Fig. 46)**. This is a five-leg track. The first leg is laid downwind, so when the dog starts it tracks along it, but when it turns 45° to the right along the second leg it is likely to track to the left. Later, when it has turned 90° to the left, it is likely to track along the right side of the third leg, and then on part of the fourth leg, until it wind-scents the track-layer, hiding some distance away behind a shed. It is interesting to watch a dog switch from a ground scent to a wind scent. As the dog is walking it gradually lifts its head, and at the same time curves as it picks up the edge of the wind-borne scent of the track-layer. It curves even more as the scent becomes stronger, and finally, when it picks up the strongest line of the scent, the dog goes straight to the person **(Fig. 47)**.

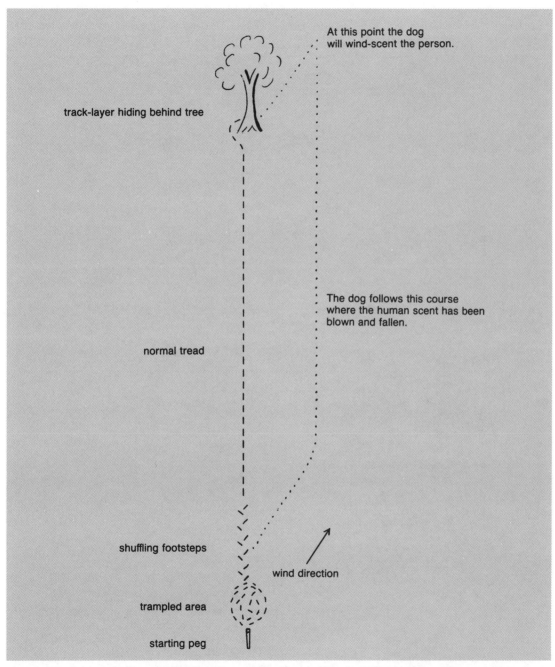

At this point the dog will wind-scent the person.

track-layer hiding behind tree

The dog follows this course where the human scent has been blown and fallen.

normal tread

shuffling footsteps

wind direction

trampled area

starting peg

Fig. 42. Body scent blown and distributed parallel to the trodden track. Soon after the start the dog is likely to track where the human scent has fallen. At the end of the track the dog is likely to go past, but then turn acutely to the left and find the track-layer.

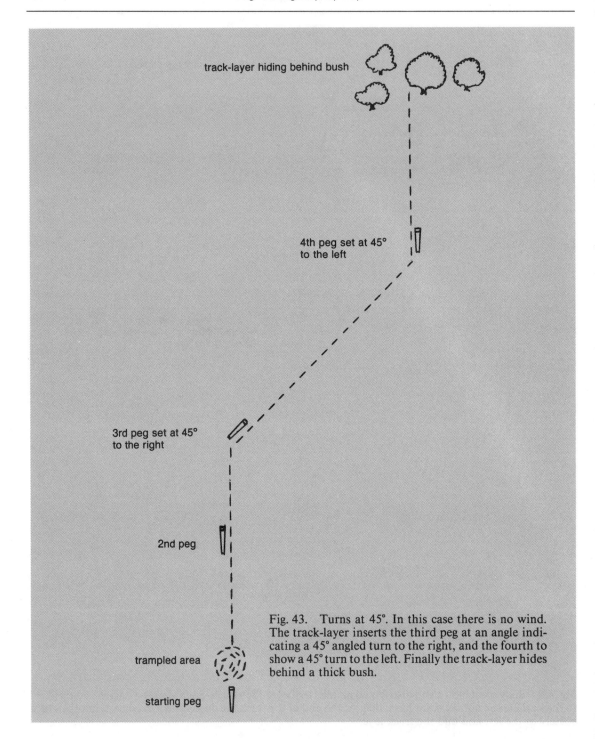

track-layer hiding behind bush

4th peg set at 45°
to the left

3rd peg set at 45°
to the right

2nd peg

trampled area

starting peg

Fig. 43. Turns at 45°. In this case there is no wind.
The track-layer inserts the third peg at an angle indicating a 45° angled turn to the right, and the fourth to
show a 45° turn to the left. Finally the track-layer hides
behind a thick bush.

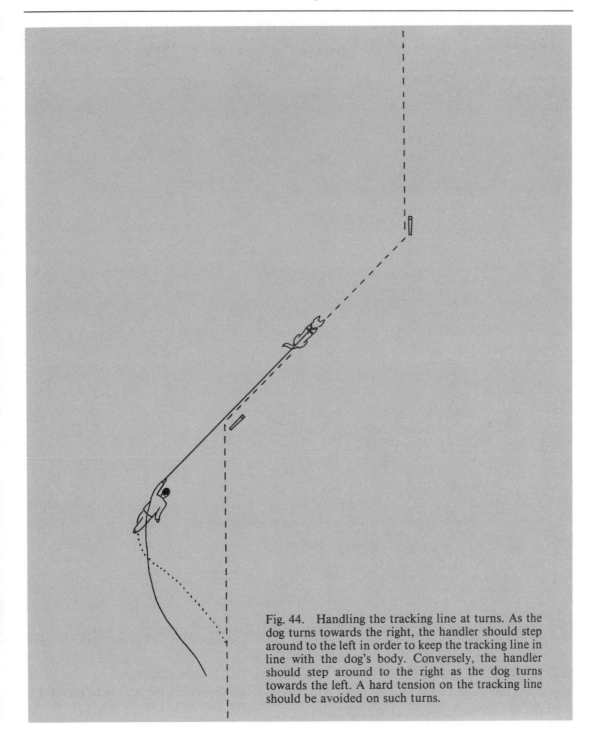

Fig. 44. Handling the tracking line at turns. As the
dog turns towards the right, the handler should step
around to the left in order to keep the tracking line in
line with the dog's body. Conversely, the handler
should step around to the right as the dog turns
towards the left. A hard tension on the tracking line
should be avoided on such turns.

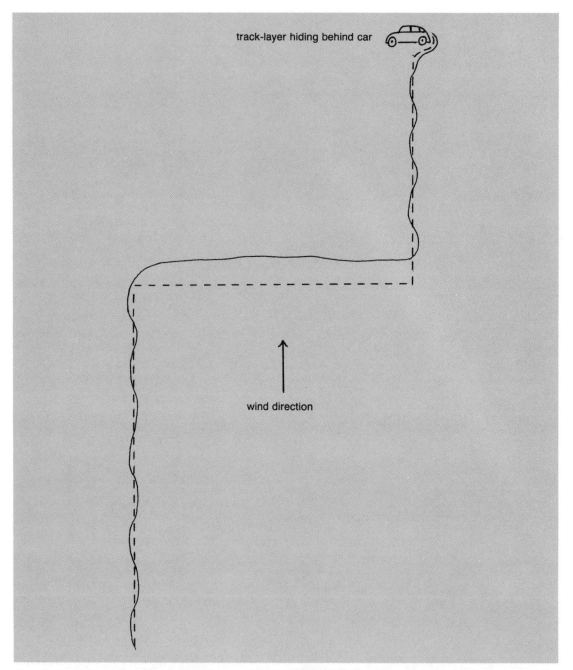

track-layer hiding behind car

wind direction

Fig. 45.   A three-legged track with 90° turns. With this track laid downwind, the dog can be expected to track straight along the first and third legs but is likely to track parallel and to the left of the second leg.

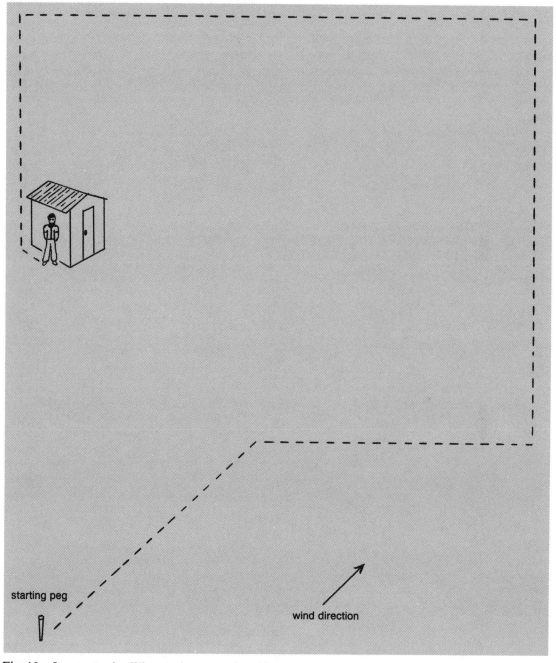

starting peg

wind direction

Fig. 46.   Longer tracks. When an instructor has drawn this track, which contains five legs and four turns, the class can be asked how they think a dog will work it.

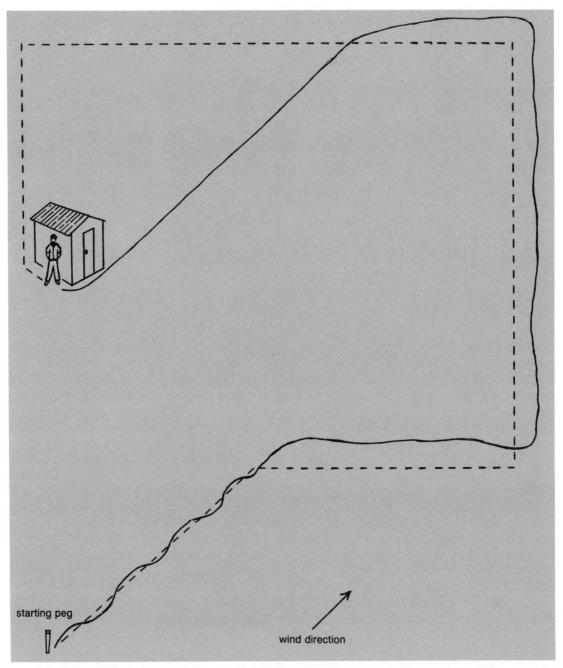

Fig. 47. The dog should track along the first leg, left of the second leg, and right of the third leg and part of the fourth leg. Then it will curve gradually to the left and lift its head, wind-scenting the track-layer a distance away behind a shed.

It is also interesting to know that even when the track-layer is hiding behind a large building, the scent will be blown around the building and straight on in the direction of the wind **(Fig. 48)**. Sometimes it can be blown around two ways, depending on the angle of the building and on the direction of the wind **(Fig. 49)**. You should never underestimate your dog's ability to wind-scent someone or something from afar. One night in 1953 I was patrolling a large airfield with my police dog when he turned positively into the wind. I knew immediately that he had picked up a scent, so I followed him. He took me straight towards the narrow gap between the huge doors of one of the hangars. We squeezed through and he took me further. It was so dark inside that I raised my other arm in front of my head, as I feared that I might walk into a propeller blade of one of the Lancaster bombers that were often inside for repairs. Suddenly he stopped. Believing that a person was unlawfully there, I challenged the intruder three times, but there was no response. I then decided to give one quick flash with my torch. I did this, and in that fraction of a second I saw the image of a body hanging in front of me with its feet about half a metre off the ground. It was a shock to me, and my immediate thought was that it was a suicide case. I put my torch on and went forward to investigate the body—and found it to be a dummy in a flying suit, suspended by a parachute which covered a frame high up. I shone my torch around the hangar and found that many such display units had been set up for the forthcoming Open Day. My dog was only interested in the dummy's flying boots, and I learnt later that the pilot who had loaned them for the display had worn them only some hours earlier. It was of great interest to me that my dog was able to pick up at a distance of about 250 metres a passive scent which had been conveyed by the wind out of the hangar and across the airfield.

descending scent

One more diagram I like to include in the lecture depicts how a dog will work when it is virtually at the end of a track and the track-layer, who had laid the track downwind, is hiding up a tree.

In most cases the dog will track to the tree and then continue tracking with its nose to the ground well past the tree—that is, it will not even sniff up the tree-trunk. Some distance past the tree, it will lift up its nose, turn around and go straight to the tree, wind-scenting and indicating to the handler that the track-layer is up there **(Fig. 50)**.

The explanation for this is quite simple. As the track-layer was climbing the tree, the natural scent from that person's body was falling and being distributed by the wind. The dog followed the *passive* scent until it picked up the *live* wind scent of the track-layer. The distance from the tree to where the dog picks up the wind scent depends on the strength of the wind and how far up the tree the track-layer is.

Handlers can learn so much from diagrams such as these, which can easily be drawn in the lecture room. I like to use large sheets of white paper for the purpose, and three bright texta colours: red for the track-layer, blue for the dog, and green for trees, buildings and the like. The advantage of drawing on sheets is that the class can refer to them again, whereas with a blackboard or whiteboard you are forever wiping the diagrams off.

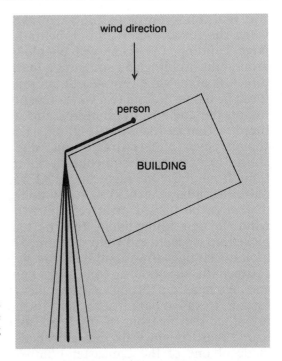

Fig. 48. Wind-borne scent. The person's scent is blown along the side of the building, then around the corner. As it continues to blow, it is fanned out, being strong in the centre but weaker on the outsides.

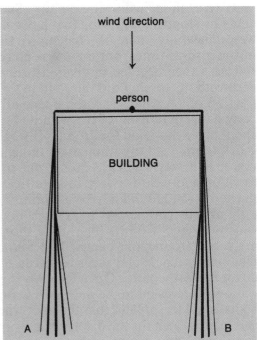

Fig. 49. Sometimes the person's scent can be blown around two sides of a building. Dogs patrolling across the wind could pick up the scent at either A or B and at great distances away, depending on the conditions.

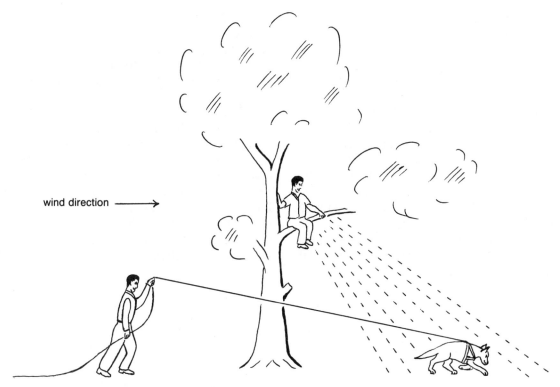

wind direction ⟶

Fig. 50. Descending scent. When a track-layer hides up a tree for some time, the human scent will descend and be blown over a certain area, as shown. The dog will track past the tree, turn around and go straight back towards the tree, wind-scenting and indicating to the handler that the track-layer is up there.

Several other very important points should be mentioned, and explained with valid reasons.

When you track, the best time of day is early in the morning when everything is cool and moist. It is ideal if there is either no wind or only a breeze, but I would avoid a strong gusty wind. A very fine rain is all right, but a strong downpour—which I cannot really imagine anyone wanting to work in anyway—is likely to wash your track away. Also, avoid extremely hot days when everything is so dry that after a time the scent will evaporate.

Foggy, misty days, when of course there is no wind, are all right, but you should wait about twenty minutes before you track with your dog. The reason is that when a track-layer walks through fog, the scent hangs in the minute molecules of water in the air. If you started to track about ten minutes after the track had been laid, your dog would probably hold its head up and sniff the air all the time. If you wait longer the scent will fall to the ground and form a more concentrated trail, which will keep the dog's nose to the ground. Snow can cover a track and preserve it, but when it thaws the scent will be washed away.

Weather and ground conditions vary from country to country—you just have to study them as you go along. I have had the opportunity of tracking in Britain, the United States and many parts of Australia, and I have found huge variations.

The best type of ground and vegetation when you first start tracking is a fairly flat and vast area with lush green grass about 5 to 8 centimetres (2 to 5 in.) high. Check for certain weeds, small as they may be. Some can be very sharp and prickly—like bindi-eye, which we have in Australia. Avoid such areas like the plague.

Always make sure that your dog is keen and alert. Never work your dog if it is off-colour or tired. Remember that a dog that has had to use its nose for any length of time can become mentally tired. It can also become very thirsty when tracking, so always carry fresh, clean drinking water for it. Before you track always ensure that your dog has had plenty of time to relieve itself. A dog cannot concentrate properly if it is uncomfortable.

And so you can see how much there is to know about this vast subject, and why I always believe in first explaining the fundamentals in a tracking lecture. It puts the handlers in good stead for the practical sessions—which, from my observations at the close of the lecture, they just can't wait to commence.

20

the first few tracks

As an instructor, I always feel that I am going to learn something new whenever I instruct a new class. Naturally I hope everything will go well, but I'm always prepared for the dog who doesn't want to track for some reason or other. It is then a case of discovering why it will not track, and then trying out different methods to get it to do so naturally.

When everyone has arrived and exercised their dogs, I ask for two or three to be brought on to the tracking area; the rest of the dogs can be put back in the cars. I would check the direction of the wind (it might be only a slight breeze), select one of the dogs to do the first track, and ask for someone known to the dog to lay the track. Let us assume the track-layer is the wife of the handler.

I would make sure I had the full attention of the class and positioned myself well, so that they could all hear me and see everything about to take place. I would then ask the track-layer to walk out about 5 or 6 metres and put the first peg in, trample around beyond it, and walk in shuffling footsteps downwind in the direction of a certain big tree behind which she was to hide. After several shuffling footsteps she could walk normally and on my direction insert three more pegs at inter-

vals. When she had hidden herself I would ask the handler to put the harness on his dog, roll out the line behind them and clip it on to the harness. As an instructor I would not just be talking to the handler but to the whole class. Having all heard the instructions so many times, they will have become very conscious of just how important good preparation is. I would also hand a clipboard to one of the members to fill in the details of every track. The handlers could take it in turns and a brief record could thus be kept of each dog's tracks during the course. (Later, each might decide to keep a home journal of tracks.) The headings on the top of the log sheet could include: date, dog's name, handler's name, track-layer's name, age of track, distance of track, ground conditions, general weather conditions, temperature, wind strength, remarks.

I would then ask the handler to stroll quietly up to the starting peg and let the dog investigate the beginning of the track, which could be about ten minutes old. I would ask the class to watch very carefully how the dog sniffed the ground:

'Look at that, everyone, see how this German Shepherd has put his nose down. See how he is investigating the area where Rosemary trampled on the ground. Oh, now watch! He's following the track on which she shuffled along. That's right, David, you stay there for a moment behind the peg, let the line run through your left hand. Your dog is straight on the track. Grip the line, and start walking. That's good. Keep your left hand up. Keep the tension and keep in line behind your dog. Handlers, do you see how the dog's tail is wagging gently from side to side? That's a good sign that he is working surely and methodically. I'll leave you now to walk with David. Watch everything on the track.'

I would keep walking with the handler, reassuring him that he was working his dog well, and if necessary giving advice. When his dog was getting near the end of the track I would advise him to let even more line run through his hand. After the dog found the handler's wife behind the tree, and they had both praised it, leash and collar would be put on and the harness taken off. We would then return to the class via another route, curving around away from the track, leaving the pegs where they were. Returning to the class that way is only a safety measure. If you return along the track, there is always the future possibility that the dog may track so far along a route and then think it is time to go back on it. However, sometimes you might have to return by the same route, and I shall deal with that in the next chapter.

When we returned to the class, I would make a few comments on the fine performance of both dog and handler, not forgetting of course the track-layer who had laid such a good track. I would also mention any particular points of interest, or ask the class if they noticed the dog quickly sniff the top of the second peg, and how very straight the dog kept. Questions would be welcomed at this point, and I would then suggest the dog be put back in

the car to rest and another handler bring a dog out, so that two or three dogs are standing by all the time. Once the instructor organises this, everyone follows the system and no time is lost.

I would then ask the next track-layer to lay a similar track about 12 metres (40 ft) from and parallel to the first track. That is why the pegs on the first track were left in the ground. It is quite a good idea to have one set in one colour and the other set in another. When the second track-layer has been found, that person can return to the class, picking up the first set of pegs to give to the third track-layer. That way there is always one set of pegs in the ground.

Now let us imagine that by the time the second track is being laid, the wind has become stronger. This time we have a Golden Retriever, who tracks as proficiently as the first dog. It is interesting to see how it wags its tail, carrying it high in a lovely gentle flowing manner like a plume on a military head-dress. Also, the dog is weaving gently from side to side in a consistent zig-zag along the track. Many dogs do this, especially when the wind is strong and blows some of the track-layer's scent to the sides of the track **(Fig. 51)**.

The third dog might be a Miniature Poodle who for some reason does not want to put its nose to the ground, despite the handler's repeated efforts to beckon the dog with her right hand to sniff the ground. Fortunately the handler can see the track-layer's footprints on the grass, which is covered in dew; this is a great help. I would advise the handler to start strolling along, so that the dog is walking straight over the footprints, in the hope that eventually it might put its nose down. If and when it does, a little bit more line should be let out, allowing the dog to use its nose and its initiative. Very often this

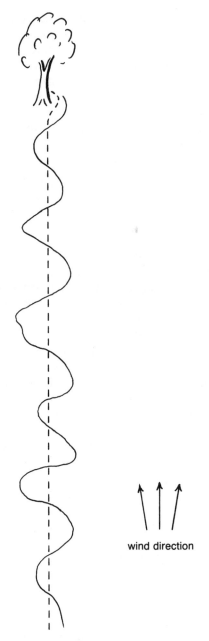

wind direction

Fig. 51. Strong winds can affect tracks. With a variable strong or gusty wind the track-layer's scent will be blown from side to side. Consequently the tracking dog will weave along, picking up the strongest scent it can.

works. But sometimes the dog may have walked about 60 metres before it puts its nose down on the 90-metre (100 yd) track. Once the dog finds the track-layer at the end of the track, it starts to get the idea of what tracking is all about; with subsequent tracks there is seldom any problem. According to one school of thought, the first track should be no more than about 30 metres long. Well, I like to start with about three times that distance, just in case I have to use that method of strolling along until the dog puts its head down.

The next dog is a male Labrador. He starts off very well and it is interesting to watch his tail: it sticks straight out and he wags it quite rapidly and horizontally. But he has one problem. As soon as he sees a tree, he wants to leave the track and rush over to lift his leg against it! This of course must be prevented. Corrections should be made immediately by pulling him away and back on to the track again; but care must be taken to avoid over-correcting, or the dog might be put off tracking.

Imagine that the next dog is a Border Collie that does not wish to put its head down and certainly won't walk out ahead, mainly because it has done a tremendous amount of heelwork. The method used on the Miniature Poodle has failed. In a case like this I would suggest that the owner let me handle the dog while he or she lays the track. In the vast majority of cases this works, for the dog just loves to find its owner. The next stage is for the owner to be accompanied by another track-layer. They can walk either side by side or one behind the other. When they have walked about 60 metres the track-layer can hide while the owner walks a further 30 metres. As the instructor works the dog, it is tracking two people at the same time. It finds the track-layer first, from whom it now receives lots of praise, and then tracks on to find its owner. This might have to be repeated a few times until the dog catches on to the idea that it has to track someone other than its owner; then the owner can work the dog.

I said earlier that it is a good idea for the handler to have the dog on the leash, and to allow it to watch the track-layer start the track and walk away to the eventual hiding-place. This sometimes presents a small problem: when the dog is taken to the starting peg, all it wants to do is walk straight down the track with its head up, using its eyesight to find the person. If this is the case, the dog should not be allowed to look. It can be put in the car while the track is being laid. The handler should watch the track being laid, and should then go and get the dog and take it to the starting peg. Now the dog will have to use its nose to find the track-layer.

I did have one extraordinary case where even that did not work. It was a German Shepherd, and for this breed not to take to tracking straight away is most unusual. It would never use its nose, but would rely totally on its eyesight to find its owner, to whom it was very attached. So the following week I got the owner together with another track-layer to lay a track without the dog seeing. Later I harnessed the dog and took it to the starting peg, while the rest of the class watched from about 30 metres away. All the dog wanted to do was stand there whining and looking around for his owner. So I stood still as well and made up my mind not to say a word. I was in fact playing a waiting game. I thought, 'Well, old boy, you want your master and you've got a nose, and I can wait!' I waited for some time, and then he put his nose to the ground, tracked for no more than

a metre, stopped and used his eyes again. I waited. After a while he did the same again. This went on and on. Every time he tracked, I would follow; every time he stopped, I stood firm. By simple trial and error he found out that we were going to advance only if he kept his nose down to the ground. Within a few minutes he was tracking with his nose down all the way and a firm tension on the line. He found the track-layer and then went on to find his owner. From that day on he never ceased to track. In fact, by the following week, not only had he caught up with the others; he was doing the turns better than any dog on the course.

Another dog I had years ago just would not put its nose down—it simply wasn't interested. Then, one day, one of the women on the course asked me if I would like her to lay the track for this particular dog that morning, because she was in the middle of her monthly period. I agreed with her that it was certainly worth a try and thanked her very much. Well, it worked! She laid two tracks for the dog that day, and the dog tracked beautifully. From then on it would track anyone. At a later date it was awarded its TD (Tracking Dog) title.

I like to have a tracking course of about eight or nine dogs, and I like each dog to have two short tracks on each of our practical working days. When they become more experienced it is best to do one long track. Having this number of people, plus any instructors and observers on the course, means that there are plenty of track-layers. And if there are both men and women, as there usually are, that is ideal, because the dogs can get used to tracking both sexes.

I never trouble to ask the class to put in cross-tracks. There are plenty of other people who do that for us as they go walking their dogs in the mornings over the different places where we track—and plenty of joggers running around too. I know that some people have a few moans and groans when, as they are tracking, other people come by exercising their dogs, but I have never had any problems with it.

Provided all the dogs are doing well during the week, the tracks laid in the next practical lesson can include 45° turns. These should be carried out as explained in the lecture on tracking (Chapter 19). In addition, an article can be placed between the second turn and where the track-layer is hiding. I always tell people not to worry if the dog does not indicate or pick up the article; the important thing is that the dog tracks. In trials dogs are required to retrieve or indicate the article, and are commonly taught to drop beside the article or sit beside it. During one of my visits to West Germany, I saw a service dog pick up an article and remain standing straight. The handler walked up and took the article, and the dog continued to track.

The following week 90° turns can be included in the tracks. It is a good idea to track on different venues every time, and the nature of the track-layers' hiding-places should also be varied. If you use trees all the time, dogs will start looking for trees, knowing that the track-layer is sure to be behind one. Use all sorts of things, so that your dog has no idea where the track-layer is hiding. It must use its nose, and you have to learn to 'read' your dog.

To read a dog really well, you have to watch everything about it—how it uses its nose, how it moves and, in particular, how it carries and wags its tail. Certain breeds have their own distinctive characteristics in this regard, but you will have to know your own dog. You can learn a lot about a dog from the way it uses its tail, and this doesn't just apply to tracking. It is unfortunate, therefore, if you have a dog without a tail! I hope that the practice of tail-docking, already in considerable disfavour, will eventually become a thing of the past.

21

progress in tracking

There seems to be no limit to what you can learn, and to the enjoyment you can derive, from the hours spent tracking with your dog. Once the basics have been taught and learnt, you can progress to tracking that is more interesting and challenging for your dog.

Whenever I am taking a class, I always select a spot where everyone can stand and watch every dog tracking, because I want them to learn as much as they can in the time we have. During the first few weeks this is very easy because the tracks are short, can be laid quickly, and do not take long to be worked; so a flat piece of land covering an extensive area is ideal. Later, the tracks need to be made gradually longer, and a little older, and to be laid in such a way as to include crossing over creeks, crawling under wire fences, going through thickly wooded areas, and other such difficulties. When we reach that stage, therefore, I like to select a spot high up, so that the class can watch a dog work downhill, cross a creek and work up the hill opposite to find the track-layer. I like to remain with the group to tell them what to watch for in particular as the dog and handler do their work. It is also good for the handler to work independently and not rely so much on the instructor. Natu-

rally, each case needs to be taken on its merits, and if I think the handler needs some advice I will follow at a distance and give help if necessary.

From this stage on I like to make the tracks really interesting for both dog and handler, and to show them all the extra things they need to do. Handlers now learn more and more about the direction of the wind and the funny tricks it can play. Some of the things I ask track-layers to negotiate, and dogs and handlers to pursue, would certainly not be heard of in tracking trials! They would be absolutely against the rules. But I like to make it challenging for the dog. Police dogs, after all, have to track through a multitude of different conditions in order to effect an arrest or find a lost person.

Let's take a simple case of a track-layer who has gone through a five-strand wire fence and straight on. When the dog detects the spot, the handler should encourage it to track under the bottom wire, proceed for about 2 metres before dropping the dog to stay (while the handler climbs through, which might take a few seconds), and then continue tracking again. This is where the obedience comes in. Similarly, take the case where a track-layer has had to cross a slippery creek with the utmost care. When the dog comes to the creek it will go straight down and climb up the other side with ease, because it has four legs and it can grip well. It is advisable in this situation for the handler to remain on the bank and let out the line as the dog goes down and up the opposite bank. When it has got there, the handler can drop it to stay, cross the creek with care, and resume tracking.

Some interesting observations can be made when dogs are tracking over creeks. The track-layer's scent can fall into pockets of soil and lie on top of still water. Also, a slight breeze can blow the scent along the creek. Consequently a tracking dog can be seen to check along the creek and return, and then pick up the track where the track-layer had crossed the creek and continued straight on.

Sometimes I have asked a track-layer to go straight towards a creek and cross it at a safe and suitable place. This may well mean turning left or right and proceeding a fair distance along the side of the creek until a suitable crossing-place is found. While the track-layer is standing there contemplating which way to go, a lot of scent is falling from that person's body and being distributed all around, even into part of the creek. Naturally, when the dog reaches that area, it can be expected to go around checking and double-checking until it proceeds along the route the track-layer eventually chose. It is therefore important that the handler remain still and wait patiently while the dog checks everything out. It is also a good idea for a peg to have been inserted on the opposite side to indicate the crossover point to the handler.

Sometimes, when everything goes as I had predicted, a member of the class might enquire curiously, 'How on earth did you know that would happen?' I then reply: 'When you have seen so many dogs of different breeds do the same sorts of things, you get to know. The dogs are showing you. All you have to do is watch and study, and read every dog like a book. With experience you too will be able to predict with a degree of certainty, though none of us will ever know it all.'

There are many things you will notice as you work tracking dogs over different types of terrain. For example, if a track is laid along the slope of a steep hill, the dog is likely to track parallel below it, because as the track-layer walks along, some of the scent will fall and land further down the slope. The wind can play some terrible tricks with scent on tracks that have been laid up, down, over and around hills. If you go for a walk over such terrain and throw up pieces of grass into the air every 100 metres or so to check the direction of the wind, you will be amazed how changeable it is. Conversely, where you have a basin-shaped piece of ground formed at the foot of two or three hills, the wind will whirl around in it. If the track-layer hides among bushes and trees in that area, his or her scent will be continuously blown around. When the dog who has just done an excellent track arrives at this basin, it will probably go around all over the place: to someone who doesn't know, it will appear to be totally confused. But given time the dog will be able to detect the source of the scent and locate the track-layer.

A track laid on still water lying in patches over a field is quite easy for a dog to follow as the scent will lie on the surface of the water; but running water will wash scent away.

A freshly ploughed field can be difficult for a dog to track on. On one occasion years ago, we worked an excellent team of German Shepherds over ground that had been greatly disturbed the day before by bulldozers clearing the land for housing. The organic smell was extremely strong (and not exactly pleasant) and all the dogs had great difficulty in working over that area. But the following week, when the smell had virtually gone, the dogs tracked the same area with absolute ease.

Once you feel that your dog is tracking extremely well, you could start introducing it to tracking on hard surfaces, like tarmac or concrete. You could start this with the track crossing over a quiet road at right-angles, with a peg inserted both sides for your guidance. Because there is no ground disturbed in crossing a road the dog must rely on the scent from the track-layer. However, there will probably be some soil particles and vegetation juices that have attached themselves earlier to the track-layer's footwear, and these will be deposited on the road as it is crossed. The track-layer can of course remove the footwear while crossing the road and walk in socked or stockinged feet—which will tend to create a better human scent.

Some of the new housing developments in and around Melbourne have provided interesting opportunities. We have laid a lot of tracks across open country and then straight through houses being constructed, proceeded over more land and finally hidden in another house nearing completion. Those who lay the tracks always ask the builders for permission, which is always happily given, and explain briefly that in about a quarter of an hour they can expect to see a dog come through, with its handler following behind on the tracking line. This sort of thing makes it very interesting for the dog, who will often scrutinise the spot where the track-layer stopped to talk to the builders, and workers who pause to watch the dogs work find it fascinating as well. It also gives the dogs practice in following a track crossed by and in the presence of strangers.

Sometimes in these areas we have been able to hide in a drain that had no cover on top. This is something new for the dog—to locate the track-layer down under ground-level. We have also had some most interesting situations where the dogs have suddenly wind-scented the track-layer and have gone straight to a closed drain, further down the road from the open drain where the track-layer was hiding. The scent had travelled underground through the pipe and come out at the other outlet!

As time goes on you should always try to put in unusual things. Before long you won't even have to take your dog up to the starting peg and say 'Find!'—it will know automatically that the harness means tracking. In fact it will often put its nose to the ground and start tracking before it even gets to the starting peg. And if it does, let it do so. Let it use its initiative; don't deter it. When your dog shows this ability, see if it will pick up the track-layer's scent when you stroll together slowly at right-angles to the track, about 10 metres from the starting peg. Often the dog will immediately drop its nose to the ground and turn quite positively in the direction of the track. If not, don't worry. Just walk on a little, turn parallel to the known track for a few paces, and turn again to cross the track for the second time. Do this slowly and keep behind the dog a bit to give it every chance to pick up the scent on the track. No-one knows how it is that dogs instinctively follow the direction in which the track-layer has gone. We just have to accept the fact that they know, just as we have to accept that pigeons instinctively know how to fly home.

Occasionally get someone your dog doesn't know to lay a track for you, and ask that person not to hide at the end of the track but to sit comfortably on a bench. Once again, you see—something different.

In the previous chapter I mentioned that sometimes it is necessary to return by the same route on which your dog tracked. Several years ago I was working with a group that was tracking in the bush. In those conditions you just have to work on a short length of line and carry the rest, otherwise you are going to get really caught up in the foliage. I laid a long track straight into the bush, and arrangements were made for the dog and handler to start tracking about half an hour later. It was a nice warm day, and having checked that there were no leeches or snakes around I lay down to have a rest; but within seconds I dropped right off to sleep. It must have been about half an hour later that I was awakened by a lick on my face from the German Shepherd who had tracked me. After we praised the dog and it had its harness removed, we decided to attempt a shortcut out of the bush to a dirt road. But we got hopelessly lost, and I don't mind admitting that it gives you a terrible feeling when you are in that position. Anyway, the handler put his dog back into harness and got it to back-track, and it took us safely out of there. So you see, so much depends on the conditions in which you are working.

As time goes on track-layers should use markers less and less, or they can use natural markers that are noted mentally by the handler. Eventually, handlers should have enough faith in their dogs to track without having any information save where the starting point is.

One day I asked a handler to note the number-plate of my car, because I was going to drive about a kilometre and a half (1 mile) down the road, park the car, lay a track and conceal a small article on the track before hiding myself. That was all— I gave no more information, because I myself didn't know where I was going!

Having parked the car on the side of the road, I climbed the high bank and walked parallel to the road. I put a small piece of wood down and covered it with a handful of grass I had plucked from the ground 2 metres away. I walked on another 20 metres and climbed high up into a tree, where I sat in a fork, koala-like, for nearly half an hour! I had a commanding view of the road, and saw the handler arrive by car, harness his dog and pick up the track from my car. The dog worked excellently all the way. When it came towards the wooden article, it veered away to sniff the spot from where I had plucked the grass. The handler, seeing the fresh grass covering the article, pulled his dog away and said, 'No, not there, stupid! Here it is.' He pointed to the article. The dog tracked on, and since there was no wind whatsoever it stopped directly underneath me. The handler waited as the dog kept sniffing the ground and then gradually lifted its nose more and more and more until it saw me, and looked at me with great interest. The handler, watching his dog, also looked up and said in amazement, 'Oh! Michael, you never told me you were going to hide up a tree!' 'Well, that's quite true,' I replied. 'From now on, it's just a case of trusting your dog.'

It was a very good track, and something completely different from what he and his dog had done before. Never before had the dog picked up the scent from a car, and never before had it detected a track-layer whose scent was descending on it. When I explained about the article, the handler realised that his dog had been right and that he should not have criticised it the way he had. Anyway, we had a good laugh about it, and it was all good experience.

So you can see what enjoyment you can have with tracking. The dog knows how to use its nose. All you have to do is channel everything in the right direction so that the dog is working for you. And don't forget: read your dog, and, above all, *trust* in your dog.

22

instructional techniques

In earlier chapters I have mentioned quite a number of instructional techniques that can be used either in training large classes of handlers or with individuals. Some techniques mentioned already include:

- Giving very brief explanations first.
- The various ways of demonstrating, i.e. using your own dog, someone else's dog, having an assistant or using an imaginary dog.
- The discreet way of taking an offered dog with which to demonstrate, and positioning yourself and the dog so that handlers can observe from the best angle.
- Positioning yourself so that you can watch the dog and your class at the same time; also, positioning yourself so that you can instruct the class of handlers working with their dogs and talk to the audience at the same time.
- Splitting the class into a working group and an audience, and then changing them around.
- Assembling a class in a straight line, and checking the collars in a few seconds.
- Preparing the class for every item in heelwork; halting the leader first so that all can form up in a straight line again.
- Training individually and at the same

time inviting all the handlers to watch and learn.
- Training in straight lines and squares as opposed to working in circles.
- Teaching new exercises based on something the handlers and dogs have already learnt.
- Teaching two exercises separately, then putting them together.
- Arranging a training programme so that everything is taught in a simple step-by-step manner to obtain the best results in the shortest time.
- Teaching the handlers how to talk to their dogs, by saying the commands with the appropriate intonations for them to copy immediately.
- Being something of a salesman in convincing handlers that it is all quite easy when you know how.

Well, that gives us quite a few techniques that can make training easy and enjoyable for all concerned. The more techniques instructors have up their sleeves, the easier they will find instructing. Better results will be achieved and fewer faults should occur.

I would now like to add to some of the above techniques and tell you about others that can and should be used.

getting across

When you are explaining something to a class, whether during a lecture in a classroom situation or outside on the training ground, maintain eye-contact. It is best to develop the habit of casting your eyes around, so that everyone feels that you, as the instructor, are interested in them as individuals and that you want to help them. When explaining make it simple. Try to avoid long words and flowery sentences, because some people will not understand you. Also, speak up so that everyone can hear. It's a good idea at the start of the lesson to ask the handlers whether they can all hear you, and to encourage them to let you know if at any time they can't hear well enough. Try to project your voice and enunciate your words clearly. When you need to speak to the class while demonstrating with a dog, be very careful that you don't talk to the ground. Sometimes it will be necessary to bend over when you are doing something with a dog. This is all right as long as you don't pick that moment to describe what you are doing; in such cases it is best to explain it before you do it.

When you are explaining it can be very helpful to use your hands in describing the way you should or should not use them on a dog. You can also use your fingers for emphasis—e.g. when stressing the four main points in the first principle of dog training (Command, Action, Response and Praise), or the four-point plan in teaching an exercise (Brief Explanation, Good Demonstration, Practical Work and Questions/Answers/Advice). Another important point: instructors should try to stand still. It can be quite distracting to see an instructor bobbing about.

I shall always remember seeing an instructor talking to a class for some time while they all stood at attention with their dogs—for one thing, he should have told them to relax, and to relax their dogs. Anyway, while he was talking he was continuously moving all over the place; in fact, he appeared to be dying to go to the toilet! I strolled on to observe the other classes, as I had been requested to do by the club, which was seeking my comments on how training methods could be improved. During the next half-hour I saw two more instructors dancing around as if they too needed to relieve themselves. It was not as if it was a cold day; on the contrary, it was very warm. When I had finished looking at the classes I asked the secretary why certain instructors were dancing around as if they wanted to go to the toilet. The secretary, somewhat amused by my comment, informed me that they did it to make themselves look busy. 'You must be joking!' I replied, and after a few seconds I couldn't contain myself any longer and burst out laughing. But the club did appreciate my suggestions, not only on this but on quite a number of other matters.

When explaining and demonstrating, always make sure you have the attention of the whole class. There are two main ways of doing this. First of all you can really capture their attention by saying, 'Now, I would like you all to listen very carefully and watch closely as I do this exercise.' Later you can say, 'I shall now demonstrate this twice, so watch carefully please.' Using the word 'twice' really makes people concentrate: they get the general idea the first time, and watch for the finer details the second time. Sometimes it is necessary to do something three or four times. In demonstrating the left turn in heelwork in a square, for example (when it is important to know how to use the left hand and foot), you can ask them to watch your left hand twice, and then watch the spin you make on your left foot twice.

Although you might have the full attention of most of the class, a few handlers could be talking or fiddling around. When this happens all you have to say is, 'Excuse me please, I wonder if I could have your attention! Thank you.' If you don't do this at the time, they will probably go on talking. Then when you have finished explaining and demonstrating they will probably, and apologetically, say, 'Oh, I missed that! Would you mind doing it again, please?' And that is really time wasted. I have heard some instructors give a very curt reply: 'Yes, I do mind! You should have been watching. Too bad!' This does nothing to foster a good relationship between the instructor and the handlers. It is much better for the instructor to secure the full attention of the class at the start. At the end of the lesson they should be thanked for their interest and cooperation. A little bit of thanks always goes a long way.

You may have given a very good explanation and demonstration, but when it comes to doing the practical work with the whole class, never expect that they are going to get it anywhere near perfect. The important thing is to convey the basic idea first, and only then to work on the finer details one at a time. Build as you go. For example, when doing heelwork with a fairly large class, you may notice that many of the handlers are pulling the leads back and up at 45° when they sit their dogs. So stress to the whole class the importance of holding the lead up at 90°. Praise the handlers for their accuracy at

the next sit. You may notice also that quite a few of the handlers are turning their feet to the left and under their dogs when they sit them. Stress the importance of keeping their feet straight on all future sits. Praise them when they get that right. Then there might be a few who are not using their left hands in the correct way, or are not bending at their knees, or are praising their dogs too vigorously, or perhaps not at all. Whatever the shortcomings, tackle them one by one every time the handlers have sat their dogs. When they have done their ninth or tenth sit, they should all know what to do and of what to be aware. If, by contrast, all such points had been mentioned at the first sit, beginners could not possibly remember them all. In fact, many would worry about all the things they were expected to do, and as a result would become tense and embarrassed if they forgot. So do it the simple way. Feed it to them gently, so that they can concentrate on one thing at a time and get it right. As time goes on it will all come together. It is very much like learning to drive a car.

Always reassure handlers who are having difficulties, and put them at ease, by saying, 'Don't worry, just have another go. You'll soon get the idea.' And every time even a little bit of progress is made, praise them and encourage them to get it even better. Many people need encouragement and support to stimulate them to keep on trying. It's amazing what an instructor can do for a handler just by giving a few words of praise and encouragement.

rapid response and correct timing
In dog training, handlers need to have or to develop very quick reflexes. Some, usually the younger ones, already have

them; but others do not. How, then, can instructors make people quicker vocally and physically and at the same time improve their powers of concentration? Well, here are two simple ways.

Let us take the first stage of the sit-stay exercise, when some dogs might suddenly get up and walk off. If the handlers are too slow in correcting their dogs (by saying 'No!', giving quick upward jerks on the leash and slackening it again), the dogs soon learn that they can get away with it, for a while at any rate. So we have to get the handlers to react immediately. Hold up something like a pencil or a bunch of keys, so that all the class can see, and ask them to say 'No!' very quickly between the time you let go of the object and the time it reaches the ground. There is not much time to say it, and they won't know when you are going to release it; so they have to concentrate 100 per cent, and have the word on the tips of their tongues. You can then do it again, holding the object a little closer to the ground and talking about something else for a while to distract them. This technique, which I developed years ago, speeds up their reflexes, improves their concentration and teaches them to ignore distractions. When they've got the idea, you can tell them to be just as quick when they have to correct their dogs —to concentrate 100 per cent by watching them and not to be distracted by other things going on around them.

Many people are not quick enough in praising their dogs as soon as they respond in the recall exercise. Arrange for the dog to sit about a metre behind a white line on a sportsfield, or behind a piece of rope lying straight along the ground. When the handler is in position to call the dog from a short distance away, tell him or her to praise it as soon as it has responded to the command 'Come!', but *before* it comes over the line or rope. This technique teaches handlers to praise dogs immediately, not only in the recall exercise but in all exercises.

The instructor very often has to be two jumps ahead of the dog and the situation, if the handler is expected to be one jump ahead. Perhaps a good example of this is seen when a dog like a Dobermann Pinscher does an extremely fast recall and it is necessary for the handler to say 'Sit!' and bring both hands up quickly to the chin when the dog is a few metres away. This often has the desired effect on the dog: it applies the brakes and comes to a screeching halt, just as dogs do in the cartoon films! But it requires very careful timing, and because the handler is not that experienced it will be necessary for the instructor to indicate when the command should be said by giving the instruction 'Now!'. The instructor will also need to know how fast the handler is in responding to that instruction. Let us imagine that the dog has been called. It responds and accelerates. When it gets within about 7 metres of the handler, the instructor says 'Now!'. By the time the handler has reacted and said 'Sit!' the dog has gone another 4 metres. It now reacts to the command and, applying the brakes, takes 3 metres to come to rest in the sit position a few centimetres in front of the handler. 'Well done! Beautifully timed!' This is an interesting exercise, and shows how the instructor has to be two jumps ahead and the handler one jump ahead: the instructor has to know how quick the handler will be and how quick the dog will be— everything is planned. There is communication from the instructor to the handler, and from the handler to the dog. And all three have to concentrate to achieve the perfect result. That's what makes dog training so interesting.

remaining flexible

All instructors need to learn how to be flexible in their approach to training different classes. It is best for an instructor to have the same class for several weeks. But sometimes this is not possible, and another instructor has to take over for one of the lessons. So much depends on the class. If it is a beginner class doing heelwork, the instructor should have them walking at a slow to moderate pace, and give detailed tuition when preparing them for every little sit and turn. If the same work is being done in the next class up, handlers and dogs can work at a slightly faster pace and all the orders can be preceded by just a little preparation—e.g. 'Get ready to halt. Handlers, halt!' In one of the top classes, handlers should all be capable of working quickly and all the orders can be specific—e.g. 'Forward!' 'Left turn!' 'Right turn!' 'Halt!'

Whatever the class, a good instructor should always remind handlers to use their number-one resource constantly when training: their eyesight. I find that many instructors in dog clubs today are expecting handlers, in the high classes at any rate, to work their dogs as if they were in obedience trials. They have to have their leashes in the left hand, and they must not talk to their dogs or even look at them until the end of every exercise when they dismiss them. In my opinion this is wrong. When you are training, you are training; you are not in a trial. If you don't have your eyes on your dog, how will you know what it is doing? So I say, keep your eyes on your dog, and if it makes an error use your voice appropriately, and your hands if necessary.

From time to time when you are instructing, show your class the *wrong* methods and give reasons why they are wrong. This is important, in case handlers are given incorrect advice by some local crackpot who professes to be an expert but in actual fact is far from it.

praise and criticism

Quite a few years ago I flew up to the north of Western Australia to hold a course for one of the dog clubs. At the evening lecture they told me that most of the handlers were experiencing a problem in the higher classes: the dogs were becoming bored, their willingness was down and they were lagging terribly. When I watched them all work the next day, I could see that this was perfectly true. So I advised them to talk to their dogs more and make every exercise enjoyable, to stroke them when they halted in heelwork, to praise them when actually doing recalls, retrieves, jumps, scent discrimination and other exercises. The dogs responded almost immediately. All they had needed was a renewal of praise and encouragement to make life fun again. They had been suffering from, if I might use the phrase, acute attacks of trialitis!

One of the most important things an instructor must do is give handlers their due praise first, before constructively criticising their faults. Let us take a handler who has told her dog to stay and walked away to do a recall. The dog is very inattentive. The handler has to call it three times before it responds. It comes very slowly. If sniffs the ground most of the way. It sits too far away in a crooked position, it goes very wide as it finishes to heel and sits in a very floppy way wagging its tail.

Now what the instructor needs to do is to look at all the good points first in order to boost the handler's ego; and then to go through the faults, giving advice on how to put them right and reassuring the handler that everything will improve. The instructor might say something like this:

'Well, Betty, do you know what I liked about your dog most? She stayed there, she came to you, and she finally finished to heel and wagged her tail. I know you had to give her three commands to come, but that was because she was inattentive. Well, I reckon you'll soon be able to overcome that. Next time you leave her, watch her and walk backwards in an irregular zig-zag pattern and then walk further away. That should really get her interest. When you call her, praise as she responds and fall down flat on your face. That should make her come fast—she'll think that you've fallen through the ground! As she comes in, mould her into the sit position and praise her. Then put the leash on so that you have better control in finishing her to heel, and use your hands to sit her straight, and praise her again. Then dismiss.'

Remarks like the above can really make the handler feel good, and encourage her to do better next time.

A less caring instructor might have said: 'Well, that's a pretty poor recall, isn't it? How long have you been training her? Eighteen months? Well, she should be much better than that. I mean, she was very inattentive, she needed three commands to come, she sniffed all the way, she sat crooked and too far away. The finish was terribly wide and then she sat floppy-like to one side. At least she came, and I guess that's the main thing. Have another go next week.'

Well, with remarks like that from an instructor, Betty just wants to go home and will probably not come back to the club. The instructor listed all the faults first, and by the time he reached the end and acknowledged that the dog had come, Betty was so upset that he might as well not have bothered. Finally he just said, 'Have another go next week.' He neither gave her any advice on how to overcome the faults, nor offered her any encouragement for the future.

questions and special attention

A good technique to improve handlers' logical reasoning is, of course, to ask questions. Naturally you would not do this in, say, the first two lessons in a beginner class; but later you can gradually put in some easy questions. As time goes on and everyone becomes more experienced, you can start asking questions that really make handlers think—about the way the dog learns, and how and why certain faults occur. They also start to realise that with careful thought and a logical approach many faults can be prevented.

Sometimes you may have one person in a class who has a fault that no-one else has, and you feel that it is right and proper to help, and to help without holding up the rest of the class. Let's take the case of one person who finds it extremely difficult to walk in a straight line but tends to walk to the left and into the poor old dog. If you arrange for that handler to stand somewhere in the middle of the class, directly facing you as the others form up in a line abreast to do heelwork, you can tell him to aim straight at you as you walk backwards. This will not only help him to walk straight, but will give confidence and prevent any feeling of awkwardness with the other members of the class.

You will often find people who don't know their left from their right. That doesn't make them silly in any way; on the contrary, they are frequently very intelligent and clever people. I told one client who had this difficulty that it was no problem as I would point in the direction I wished her to go. I learnt later that she could write with both hands. Being a schoolteacher, she found this to be a great advantage when at the blackboard, as she could turn around either way to watch the children as she was writing.

There is a very simple technique you can use when the whole class is walking abreast of each other and you want them to turn left. As you say 'Get ready for a left turn', point with your right hand to the right and say 'Left turn!'. (Just remember that their left is your right, because you are facing them.) When you want them to halt you can put both hands up; when you want them to come forward you can beckon them with both hands towards you; and when you want them to about-turn you can point towards the class with both index fingers. These signals can always be used on a windy day, when a lot of people might have difficulty hearing.

Quite often handlers will have some particular difficulty with their dogs, or just find some exercises difficult to do. If such problems arise it is best to ask the handlers in question if they would care to remain behind after the class has finished. You will usually find that they will more than welcome your offer, appreciating your interest and willingness to help them and understanding that it isn't exactly practicable to hold up the class just for them. Anyway, they will probably feel more at ease seeing you alone after the class than trying to overcome their problem in front of the others.

anticipation

When dogs have been trained for quite a few weeks, some of them become very smart and start to anticipate what their handlers are going to say and do. Either they pick up the clue from the order given by the instructor (e.g. 'Class, forward!'), or they learn by the sequence and timing adopted from one exercise and the next. You will usually see it first happen in Class II or III. When the instructor says 'Class forward!' before the handlers have said 'Heel!', some of the dogs will anticipate and get up and move forward. A very simple technique can be applied to correct this. The instructor should tell the class what has been observed, and ask them to remain quite still at the next 'Class, forward!': if any of the dogs get up, the handlers should promptly sit them again. They might have to do this a few times, until in the end the over-eager dogs will learn that they have to wait for the command 'Heel!' and for the handler to step forward before they are allowed to move off from the sit position. Anticipation can occur in any exercise, and this technique can be applied to them all.

I would like to close with an amusing story on that subject. In 1954 I was assisting an instructor, Corporal Harry Fox, on one of the courses at the RAF Police Dog Training Centre. He noticed that the handlers (not just the dogs) were anticipating the right-about turn when doing obedience on the parade ground. The order given was 'Turning about, about . . . turn!' and, as with most orders in the services, the cautionary words came first, and then a few seconds later the executive word of command. Well, Harry marched them across the parade ground, called out 'Turning about, about . . .' and then— nothing. They wondered what had happened, but he let them walk on for some considerable distance with their dogs before finally yelling out 'Turn!'. As they came back he turned to me and said with a chuckle, 'There you are, a simple technique. That'll stop 'em anticipating!'

23

qualities of a good instructor

The qualities of a good instructor are many and they vary in degree and performance. None of us is, or ever will be, perfect, but what we should all strive to do is our best. I don't think anyone could ask for more than that.

Over the many years that I have been instructing people and training dogs, I have had the opportunity and great pleasure of working with many instructors, in the Royal Air Force, in the guide-dog associations and in various dog-training clubs. I have also had numerous opportunities overseas to watch instructors and discuss many things with them in their respective places of employment, such as guide-dog training centres, police-dog centres and customs-dog centres. All of that experience has been invaluable.

I can honestly say that the vast majority of the instructors had very fine qualities—some more than others of course. I have also met some very good instructors in obedience dog-training clubs, but regrettably I have met some who were not very good—and a few who, in my opinion, should not have been instructing in such places.

Some who were brilliant at training dogs were not so good at instructing people. In many cases this was because they did not have the ability to impart their knowledge to others. On the other hand, some instructors who had not achieved high awards with their own trained dogs were extremely good at teaching others. You will see this in many fields of human activity, especially in sport.

How does one become an instructor? Why does one want to instruct in the first place? What makes a good instructor? Where does one start? What are the necessary qualifications? There is no single answer to any of these questions. Much depends on the situation and the circumstances.

Naturally, we are looking for people who are interested in training dogs, observing their behaviour, studying canine psychology, and instructing and helping the handlers.

An instructor should be sound in temperament, because he or she will have to deal with a variety of situations; and should be a patient, understanding, considerate and sincere person—one who can be gentle with sensitive people, sympathetic with people experiencing distress, firm and tolerant with difficult people, and tactful enough not to upset anyone.

An instructor should always be ready to praise handlers on their achievements, encourage those who feel defeated and instil confidence in everyone, especially those who are shy, hesitant or lack confidence.

An instructor should develop the art of explaining things briefly, be a good demonstrator, have the ability to cope with large numbers and at the same time be willing to give individual tuition. When explaining, an instructor should use simple language with the aid of hand-movements, especially if there are new migrants in the class who are experiencing language difficulties. Some handlers may have had very little formal education but have a high aptitude for dog training. All that is required is a simple explanation to everything.

An instructor should be relaxed and should convey this to the class. He or she should have—or try to develop—a good voice, quick reflexes, a watchful eye, the ability to organise and the art of correct timing.

An instructor should know how to keep handlers interested and active, endeavour to set a high standard, study and experiment with new techniques, have a knowledge of the obedience trial book, be willing to give further time if possible at the close of the class to those who need it, and show the wrong ways of doing things with valid reasons why they are wrong.

An instructor should develop the technique of handling a strange dog, always reserving the right to refuse to do so in a class situation if the dog is nervous or aggressive. (By the same token, the handler should have the right to refuse the instructor permission to handle his or her dog.)

An instructor should have the ability to make a final decision in respect of dangerous, uncontrollable or untrustworthy dogs. Handlers of such dogs should be politely and tactfully informed by the instructor, usually the chief instructor, that in the interests of all concerned it is respectfully requested that the dog not be brought for training again. However, it should always be added that the club would welcome the handler back with another dog.

An instructor should plan the programme for each training session, and should always allocate time for questions, answers and advice. If a question is asked to which the instructor does not know the answer, he or she should admit it and promise to try to find out—and should then stand by that promise. If, after extensive enquiries, an answer cannot be found, the handler should be informed of this or be told that enquiries will continue to be made.

An instructor should also be prepared to train children. Sometimes children will need a bit of a helping hand, but often they appear to be brighter than some adults, mainly because they are living in a continuous learning environment at school.

Every instructor should politely set out a few rules when starting to train a beginner class: that handlers should not smoke while training, that all dogs must be on their leashes (explaining that only in the higher classes can they be taken off, when permission is given), and that all handlers are to be responsible for picking up their dogs' droppings.

An instructor should always attempt to be fresh and alert when taking a class—

not tired, or suffering from an over-indulgence the night before, for this will show in the performance. Nor should an instructor be like a sergeant-major, drilling handlers as if they were soldiers on a parade ground.

From time to time and in certain places, dogs are being puppy-walked as future guide dogs for the blind or potential police dogs. They are sometimes brought to obedience clubs by their walkers, mainly for socialisation but also for a little bit of basic training. It is important that instructors be flexible with these dogs. In the case of dogs being reared as guide dogs, strict heelwork is to be avoided or it may deter the dog from leading out in its future work. Also, certain commands may be different—for example, a guide dog may be told 'Stop!' instead of 'Stand!'.

Well, I sincerely hope that those interested in taking up instructing will not be put off after reading this chapter. On the contrary, I hope that they will feel more positive towards taking it up, and that the points I have mentioned will be of guidance to them. Naturally, many of these things develop with experience, and most instructors will tell you that their confidence grew with experience. In return for everything that an instructor puts into the work, he or she should earn the respect and affection of all who pass through the classes; and the reward of seeing people so happy with the training they and their dogs have received is immeasurable.

Finally, might I say that one of the greatest natural qualities an instructor should possess and cherish is a sense of humour. I think it is true to say that most of us 'doggy' people have a good sense of humour. In any case, never forget that there is nearly always a funny side to even the most serious things in life.

24

handlers' attributes

When new handlers have joined a beginner class, it is important for the instructor to observe the particular attributes each handler has. While some of these attributes may be naturally very good, others may need to be improved if the best results are to be achieved. Important attributes would include:

- having a good understanding of a dog;
- having a right attitude to training;
- having good vocal and physical control;
- having quick reflexes and good powers of concentration, and being alert, attentive and confident.

The instructor will be able to find out more about the handler soon after the actual training has begun. If a dog has been difficult to start with, but has improved during the next few weeks, it is obvious that the handler has persevered conscientiously and consistently in training the dog daily. If the same dog has not made progress, it should be the job of the instructor to encourage the handler to persevere, and to give assurance that everything should improve.

The instructor should soon find out how well the handler understands the dog. In most cases experienced dog-owners have a fairly good understanding of their dogs. But it can be hard for a handler who has never had a dog before. This is where the instructor can help enormously, by showing the handler how the dog will respond to the different ways of being talked to and handled. The instructor can teach the handler how to read the dog by watching how it uses its nose, ears and eyes, its general body-movements, and the variety of ways in which it wags its tail in different situations.

Within a few lessons it is interesting to observe the handler's attitude towards the dog, the training and the instructor. I believe there has to be a good relationship between instructor, handler and dog if success is to be achieved in training. It is like a triangle. The inside of the triangle represents Training. The three points of the triangle represent Instructor, Handler and Dog, and the three sides of the triangle represent the relationship between all three.

As a few more weeks pass by, an instructor can really gauge the degree of keenness shown by the handler, and also that person's adaptability to dog training .

I think it's reasonable to say that most people who take up dog training have a fair degree of confidence; but there are quite a few people lacking in it. Once again, it is up to the instructor to try to instil confidence in the handler. A lack of confidence might be clearly seen when a handler is going to do the first sit-stay with the dog on a leash, and hesitatingly, with a very shaky request to the dog, asks 'Stay?' —as if to say '*Please* stay there'. And although the instructor tells the handler to leave the dog, the handler more or less freezes on the spot. Then, after the instructor has again told the handler to leave the dog, the dog moves: the handler's hesitancy has quickly been transmitted to it. When this happens it is necessary for the instructor to demonstrate again, this time with an imaginary dog, the manner of saying quite positively the word 'Stay!'. It is an imperative command with an exclamation mark after it—not a half-hearted request trailing a question mark. The instructor should then demonstrate how, as soon as the command has been given, the handler should confidently and positively leave the dog. It is amazing what that extra bit of tuition will do. Perhaps for the first time, the handler will realise the importance of being positive and appearing confident.

It is very seldom indeed that you get a person who is over-confident. I have had a few such people, mostly handlers who had done a fair amount of training, but the standard of their work has not been good. They have also tended to be cocky, and always ready to blame their dogs and not themselves.

When I asked one such handler if he could do a recall, he answered, rather bluntly, 'Yes of course I can.' So I asked him if he would tell his dog to sit and stay and leave the dog. This he did, but soon after he walked away his dog got up and followed him. Normally, I would tell a handler that the dog had got up, but because of this man's cocky attitude I decided not to. When he had walked about 30 metres I asked him to about-turn and halt. As he did so, there to his annoyance was his dog standing in front of him. I quietly asked him to bring his dog back to where he had told it to stay, and that we would start again. But before we did, I told him that from the way the dog had reacted I could tell that he had had some trouble with the exercise, and he confessed that this was so. 'Never mind,' I said, 'have another go, but this time keep your eyes on your dog the whole time as you walk away and be ready to correct it immediately should it move.' Sure enough, it moved again. The handler corrected it, and had another go at the recall. Third time lucky: the dog stayed, and came when called. I congratulated him on a job well done, and I believe the incident taught him not to be so over-confident and cocky, for he never acted that way again during the course. Incidentally, everyone else on the course who was watching kept quiet when the dog walked after the handler. They caught on very quickly that I was allowing something to go wrong, and that I had a very special reason for it on that occasion.

Over the years, I have become very interested in the professions and occupations of my clients, and have found that what they do in their daily work usually has a great bearing on their handling and training of their dogs. The many nursing sisters I have worked with have all had one characteristic in common: a sense of caring. I also have a lot of secretaries, accountants and office workers, and the common trait among them is efficiency: they work methodically, and they do the same with their dogs. Then there are men and women from the armed services, the police force and the fire brigade: the common factor they share is discipline, and their footwork is perfect.

Recently I had an airline pilot who trained very well with his dog. I only had to show him something once and he got it right. Whenever I asked him to sit his dog, he checked everything out, prepared well and brought his dog into a perfect sit position—a perfect landing, as it were! It was marvellous.

Several years ago I visited a woman who was four months pregnant and she wanted me to train her with her German Shepherd, to give her more control over the dog by the time her baby arrived. Well, she did very well and her bitch was very receptive. When I visited her the following week I was surprised to hear that when she spoke to her dog, her voice was just like mine. It is well known that handlers will often take on the voices of their instructors after several weeks; but I had given her only one lesson. Then she told me what she did for a living—she was an actress!

I have quite a number of boys and girls, from about ten years upwards, who come for training. The girls nearly always outshine the boys, because they mature earlier. Often when I get to the end of the first lesson, I will say to a girl who has learnt very well, 'Am I right in assuming that you have a horse or a pony at home?' With a surprised look on her face she says, 'Yes, I have. How did you know?' 'It's the way you've handled the dog. I can see you have a natural rapport with animals.'

With the boys that are very good I ask an entirely different question, and I always ask it in front of the boy's parent or parents: 'Am I correct in assuming you are good at maths and science subjects at school?' 'Yes,' his parents will reply. 'He's nearly always top of his class in maths and science.' The reason why I don't ask the boy on his own is that he might feel a bit shy and modest about telling me how good he really is, and may just pass it off by saying that he is OK at those subjects.

You may well ask what being good at maths and science has to do with training dogs. I queried this many years ago when I was interviewed by the late Capt. N. Liakhoff, MBE, Director of Training in the Guide Dogs for the Blind Association in England. He had been very interested to see, on my application form, that I had a liking for maths and physics. When I asked him why, he replied: 'If a person is good at maths, he must be able to work out problems logically. And trainers will always be faced with problems in training handlers and dogs.' That was one of the many things I learnt from him and since then I have found it to be very true. People such as scientists, doctors and accountants have generally excelled in learning how to train their dogs.

Last year I trained a woman with her dog in just five lessons. She was an excellent handler and her dog was most receptive. All I knew about her was that she was married and had a little girl. Her vocal control was excellent, she had perfect footwork, handwork, timing and coordination, and she knew how to use her body. She was so relaxed and everything flowed so smoothly. It seemed to me that whatever job she had must have had a great bearing on the training with her dog. So I asked her what she did for a living. 'Well,' she answered quite openly, 'I have a part-time job. I'm a stripper.' She also told me she was a singer, which accounted for her good voice.

25

to conclude

Years ago I would never have thought that dog training, which started as a pure hobby for me, would become my life's work, let alone that I would ever write books on the subject. And who would have thought that dog training was going to grow and expand to the scale it has assumed today in many countries.

In writing this book I have tried to convey to my readers just how interesting, rewarding and easy dog training really is, and at the same time to show what a joy and a pleasure it can be to own a happy, well-behaved pet. I hope that what I have written will be of help to handlers and instructors. There always seems to be so much to write about, but of course it is impossible to get it all into one book. The little stories I have told are just a few of the many I could recount, but I hope they have helped to illustrate what I have been saying.

It is wonderful to see so many dog clubs operating today, and the one thing they all want is more and more instructors, and good ones. I have always felt indebted to the instructors who helped me in the past, and it has therefore given me much pleasure to help others train their dogs. The success of a dog-training club depends largely on the instructors and the instruc-

tion they give. Furthermore, the instructors who take the beginner classes should be among the most experienced in the club. It is so important that new handlers and dogs receive the best tuition they can get, for their future depends largely on what they are taught in their first weeks of training. Naturally, these very experienced instructors are also needed for the higher classes. With so many more advanced exercises required to be taught in those classes, there have to be knowledgeable instructors to teach them. So aspiring instructors, or those with only a certain amount of experience, should take the classes in between, such as Class II or III. When they have gained more experience they will feel more confident about taking beginner classes and later the higher classes.

The success of the club also depends upon handlers, who should support their instructors and show their appreciation for the fine tuition they receive by working hard at home during the week and striving to produce their best. I believe that the key to success is to get the basics well established first, erecting a solid foundation that can be built upon. I also believe that we should always be striving to improve our training methods. New techniques should be looked at sensibly and objectively. If they work and you get good or better results, why not adopt them? If they don't work you can discard them, but at least you can say you tried them out.

Although I have said a lot about the basics in obedience training, I hope that I have whetted your appetite to go further by teaching your dog to do extra things like retrieving, or by going in for agility and trick work, or even by working in demonstration teams. On the other hand, you may like to take up competitive work by training for and entering obedience and tracking trials. Choose what you would like to do. Even if you don't want to go in for trials, you can still have a lot of fun training your dog to do some of the exercises.

You don't have to enter trials in order to gain experience in that area: you may like to form small groups and work on similar lines to those I suggested earlier. There is no limit to what you can do, and you can have a very enjoyable time doing it. You can relax completely doing something like that, whereas you might not be the kind of person who can relax if competing in a trial. Just get out there and enjoy yourself. It's very nice to win awards, but awards are not everything. I have been into the homes of some handlers who are always attending trials and shows, and they have so many trophies that there is hardly any room to put anything else!

A few years ago a chief instructor of a well-known police-dog training establishment was asked if he had ever received any awards for his services. He replied, 'No, not as such. All my awards are on four feet serving the community.' Those police dogs and their handlers meant a great deal to him and he had ample reason to be proud of every one of them.

So in closing, it only remains for me to wish you well with your dogs, and success in all the training you do with them. Look after them, love them, teach them, watch them, read them, talk to them. And above all, cherish their loyal companionship and devotion.

appendix

Australian National Kennel Council
Royal Show Grounds
Epsom Road
Ascot Vale VIC 3032
Australia

The American Kennel Club
51 Madison Avenue
New York NY 10010
USA

The Kennel Union of Southern Africa
6th Floor, Bree Castle
68 Bree Street
Cape Town 8001
South Africa

The Kennel Club
1 Clarges Street
Piccadilly
London W1 Y8AB
United Kingdom

New Zealand Kennel Club (Inc.)
Private Bag
Porirua
New Zealand

The Canadian Kennel Club
100-189 Skyway Avenue
Etobicoke
Ontario M9W 6R4
Canada

index